FOREST BATHING

FOREST BATHING

HOW TREES CAN HELP YOU FIND
HEALTH AND HAPPINESS

DR. QING LI

VIKING

VIKING

An imprint of Penguin Random House LLC
375 Hudson Street
New York, New York 10014
penguin.com

Maps by Sarah Locher
Graphs by Michael Davis

ISBN: 9780525559856 (hardcover)
ISBN: 9780525559863 (ebook)

Printed in the United States of America
10   9   8   7   6   5   4   3   2

Neither the publisher nor the author is engaged in rendering
professional advice or services to the individual reader. The
ideas, procedures, and suggestions contained in this book
are not intended as a substitute for consulting with your
physician. All matters regarding your health require medical
supervision. Neither the author nor the publisher shall be
liable or responsible for any loss or damage allegedly arising
from any information or suggestion in this book.

To my daughter Lulu Li, my wife Zhiyu Wang, and my parents, Yuxing Li and Jinhua Yuan

Dr. Qing Li is Associate Professor at the Nippon Medical School in Tokyo; he is one of the world's leading experts on forest-bathing. Dr. Li is vice-president and the secretary general of the International Society of Nature and Forest Medicine and the president of the Society of Forest Medicine in Japan. He is also one of the directors of the Forest Therapy Society in Japan.

Contents

Appendices

SOME FOREST THERAPY BASES IN JAPAN

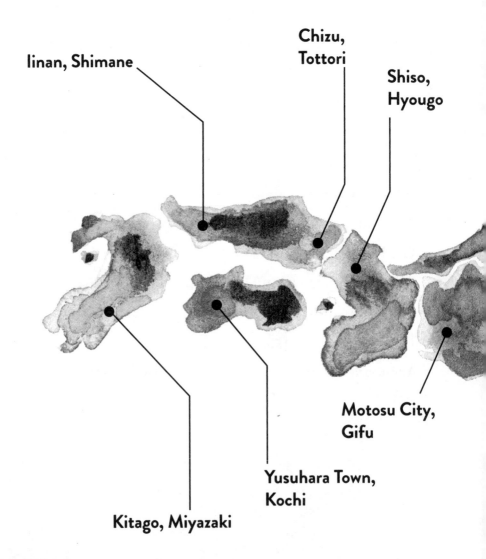

Iinan, Shimane

Chizu, Tottori

Shiso, Hyougo

Motosu City, Gifu

Yusuhara Town, Kochi

Kitago, Miyazaki

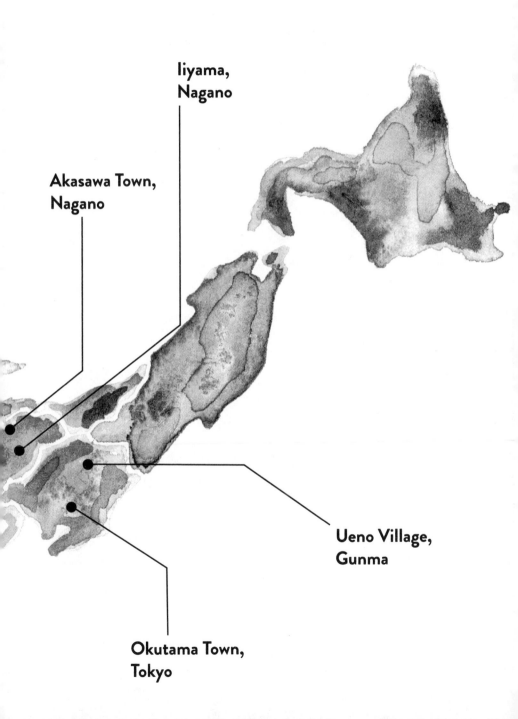

Iiyama,
Nagano

Akasawa Town,
Nagano

Ueno Village,
Gunma

Okutama Town,
Tokyo

Our Relationship to Forests

We all know how good being in nature can make us feel. We have known it for millennia. The sounds of the forest, the scent of the trees, the sunlight playing through the leaves, the fresh, clean air — these things give us a sense of comfort. They ease our stress and worry, help us to relax and to think more clearly. Being in nature can restore our mood, give us back our energy and vitality, refresh and rejuvenate us.

We know this deep in our bones. It is like an intuition, or an instinct, a feeling that is sometimes hard to describe. In Japanese, we have a word for those feelings that are too deep for words: *yūgen*. *Yūgen* gives us a profound sense of the beauty and mystery of the universe. It is about this world but suggests something beyond it. The playwright Zeami Motokiyo describes it as the 'subtle shadows of bamboo on bamboo', the feeling you get when you 'watch the sun sink behind a flower-clad hill' or 'when you wander in a huge forest without thought of return'.

I feel this way when I am in
nature. I think of my childhood
in a small village. I remember the
green poplar forests in spring and
summer and the yellow leaves in
autumn. I recall the games of hide
and seek I played in the trees with
my friends and the animals we
used to find, like rabbits and foxes,
Chinese hamsters and squirrels.
There was a beautiful apricot
forest in my village which flowered
pink all through April. I can still
remember the taste of the apricots
we harvested in the autumn.

But what exactly is this feeling that is
so hard to put into words? What lies
behind it? How does nature make us
feel this way? I am a scientist, not a
poet. And I have been investigating
the science behind that feeling for
many years. I want to know why we
feel so much better when we are in
nature. What is this secret power
of trees that makes us so much
healthier and happier? Why is it that
we feel less stressed and have more
energy just by walking in the forest?
Some people study forests. Some
people study medicine. I study forest
medicine to find out all the ways
in which walking in the forest can
improve our well-being.

When was the last time you
strolled in a forest or walked through
woodland so beautiful it made you
stop and marvel? When did you last
notice the spring buds unfurling or
look closely at the frost patterns on a
winter leaf? I wonder, instead, how
many hours you spent looking at a
screen today, and how many times
you checked your phone. In your
air-conditioned or heated office,
you might not even have noticed the
weather. You could have missed the
changing of the seasons altogether.
Did you realize that it's spring outside?
That autumn has turned?

I no longer live in the countryside. I now
live in Tokyo, one of the largest cities
in the world – and the one with the
most people. From a little fishing port
in the old Musashi province, Tokyo has
grown into the most crowded city in
the world, with a population of around
thirteen and a half million. That is about
11 per cent of Japan's total population.
And we are crammed into 2,191 square
kilometres, or 0.06 per cent of the
total area of Japan. In other words, in
Tokyo, there are 6,158 people per square
kilometre. As a comparison, London has
1,510 inhabitants per square kilometre,
Paris 2,844 and New York 1,800.

But I am lucky. I work right next to a
park with a famous shrine where there
are lots of trees. From my office window
I can see beautiful scenery and I walk in
the shrine at lunchtime almost every day.

There are huge gingko trees, cherry
trees and a 300-year-old azalea
garden with thousands of different
varieties, some with tiny flowers,
like the Fuji-tsutsuji, and some with
flowers as big as wheels, like the
Hanaguruma. They flower in April
and May in shades of deep red, pink
and white. I love to see the cherry
trees blossom and, as the summer
moves on, I enjoy the many different
shades of green. In the autumn,
the leaves of the gingko change to a
dramatic yellow. There was a delicious
calming breeze when I went for my
walk at lunchtime today and I noticed
that, yes, the gingko is beginning to
get its lovely autumnal colour. At the
weekends, I visit the green parks of
Tokyo and spend several hours there.
And every Monday afternoon I take
my students for a walk.

The Nezu Shrine in Tokyo is one of Japan's oldest shrines

Actually, this is more than just a walk. We are practising what we in Japan call forest-bathing, or *shinrin-yoku*. *Shinrin* in Japanese means 'forest', and *yoku* means 'bath'. So *shinrin-yoku* means bathing in the forest atmosphere, or taking in the forest through our senses. This is not exercise, or hiking, or jogging. It is simply being in nature, connecting with it through our sense of sight, hearing, taste, smell and touch. Indoors, we tend to use only two senses, our eyes and our ears. Outside is where we can smell the flowers, taste the fresh air, look at the changing colours of the trees, hear the birds singing and feel the breeze on our skin. And when we open up our senses, we begin to connect to the natural world.

The leaves of the gingko tree turn a distinctive bright yellow colour in autumn

Biophilia hypothesis

The concept that humans have a biological need to connect with nature has been called biophilia, from the Greek, meaning 'love of life and the living world'. The concept was made popular by the American biologist E. O. Wilson in 1984. He believed that, because we evolved in nature, we have a biological need to connect with it. We love nature because we learned to love the things that helped us to survive. We feel comfortable in nature because that is where we have lived for most of our life on earth. We are genetically determined to love the natural world. It is in our DNA.

And this affinity for the natural world is fundamental to our health. Contact with nature is as vital to our well-being as regular exercise and a healthy diet. 'Our existence depends on this propensity, our spirit is woven from it, hope rises on its currents,' wrote Wilson. We are 'hard-wired' to affiliate with the natural world — and just as our health improves when we are in it, so our health suffers when we are divorced from it.

We are part of the natural world. Our rhythms are the rhythms of nature. As we walk slowly through the forest, seeing, listening, smelling, tasting and touching, we bring our rhythms into step with nature. Shinrin-yoku is like a bridge. By opening our senses, it bridges the gap between us and the natural world. And when we are in harmony with the natural world we can begin to heal. Our nervous system can reset itself, our bodies and minds can go back to how they ought to be. No longer out of kilter with nature but once again in tune with it, we are refreshed and restored. We may not travel very far on our forest walk but, in connecting us with nature, shinrin-yoku takes us all the way home to our true selves.

Shinrin-yoku is like a bridge. By opening our senses, it bridges the gap between us and the natural world.

Why Japan?

It is no surprise that shinrin-yoku developed
in Japan. The Japanese are a forest civilization.
Their culture, philosophy and religion are
carved out of the forests that blanket the
country – not to mention all manner of
everyday things, from houses and shrines to
walking sticks and spoons.

Two thirds of the country is covered in
forest. It may be one of the most densely
populated countries in the world, but it
is also one of the greenest, with a huge
diversity of trees. If you fly over Japan, you
will be amazed to see how green it is:
3,000 miles of forest, from subarctic
Hokkaido in the north to subtropical Okinawa
in the south, with the Japanese Alps in the
middle, a spine of forested mountains known
as the Roof of the Island. It is sometimes
referred to as the green archipelago. The only
other countries with similar amounts of forest
are Finland and Sweden, and they are much
less densely populated.

Perhaps the most famous Japanese tree
is the *sugi*, or Japanese cedar, which is
like the redwoods and giant sequoias of
California. These trees can live for over a
thousand years and reach heights of up
to fifty metres with a girth of up to ten.
They grow very straight, and the name
sugi is thought to come from the word
mallugu-ki or 'perfectly straight tree'.

One of the world's oldest trees is a *sugi*, the Jomon sugi on Yakushima island, a small island off the south of Kyushu, which is home to some of the best-preserved temperate rainforests in Japan. The Jomon sugi is thought to be between two and five thousand years old. Some experts think it might even be seven thousand years old.

The Jomon sugi is located on the island of Yakushima

Both of Japan's official religions —
Shinto and Buddhism — believe that
the forest is the realm of the divine.
For Zen Buddhists, scripture is
written in the landscape. The natural
world itself is the whole book of
God. In Shinto, the spirits are not
separate from nature, they are in it.
They are in the trees, in the rocks, in
the breeze, the stream, the waterfall.
These spirits are called *kami*. There are
millions and millions of *kami*. They
can be everywhere in nature. And the
places where gods live can become
the places of worship themselves. It
is not unusual in Japan to find people
worshipping in the forest.

For Zen
Buddhists,
sculpture
is written
in the
landscape.
The natural
world itself
is the whole
book of God.

There is a story in the *Chronicles of Japan*, the second-oldest book in Japanese history, which explains why the country is so full of trees. One day, the storm god Susanoo-no-Mikoto plucked one of the hairs from his beard and transformed it into a *sugi* tree. Then he plucked a hair from his breast and turned it into a cypress tree. He took one from his buttock and turned that into a black pine tree, and one from his eyebrow, which he turned into a laurel. Then he ordered his children Itakeru-no-Mikito, Ohyatsu-hime and Tsumatsu-hime to spread the trees throughout the land. And that is how Japan became so green.

Many Japanese folk stories are about *kodama*, a kind of nature deity that lives in a tree, a bit like a Greek dryad. Some people believed that *kodama* travel about the forest, moving from tree to tree. Others believed they inhabit a particular tree. Knowledge of the trees that have *kodama* living in them is passed down through the generations, and those trees are protected. If you cut down a tree that has a *kodama* living in it, you will be cursed. The most famous *kodama* are the little white creatures with large heads and round black eyes and mouths in the *anime* film *Princess Mononoke*, which tells of an epic struggle between mankind and nature. As the forest is dying, the *kodama* fall from the trees and dissolve. And when, in the end, the forest is restored, a single *kodama* floats out of the undergrowth, rattling its head.

Many Japanese folk stories are about *kodama,* a kind of nature deity that lives in a tree, a bit like a Greek dryad.

Nature is not separate from mankind in Japanese culture. It is part of us. And the need to keep the two in harmony can be seen in every aspect of life, from the design of gardens that incorporate the natural landscape to the design of houses that blur inside and outside by means of translucent paper screens. In traditional Japanese houses you can close the door without shutting out the sound of the birds singing or the rustle of the breeze.

Shizen — which translates as 'nature', or 'naturalness' — is one of the seven principles of Zen aesthetics. The idea behind shizen is that we are all connected to nature, emotionally, spiritually and physically; and that the more closely something relates to nature, the more pleasing it is, whether it's a spoon, or a piece of furniture, or the way a house is decorated. The patterns on a kimono are often of the natural world, so that you can be wrapped in peonies or wisteria, cherry blossom or chrysanthemums, even whole landscapes of rivers, trees and mountains.

Ikebana

The Japanese art of flower-arranging

The Japanese art of flower-arranging is called ikebana. It is also known as Kadō, or the way of flowers. It is counted as one of the three Japanese arts of refinement, together with Kōdō (the way of incense) and Sadō (the way of tea). Ikebana is more than simply putting flowers in a vase. It is a disciplined art form that draws nature and humanity together and merges the indoors with the outdoors. The spiritual aspect of the way of flowers is also very important. Ikebana is a meditative practice, which gives us space and silence in which to consider the passing of the seasons and to appreciate the things in nature we are often too busy to notice in our everyday lives. To convey as natural an impression as possible, an ikebana arrangement includes not just flowers but also leaves and branches. A low, open vase leaves the surface of the water exposed and creates the effect of a plant in its natural environment. The placement of even a single flower should take into consideration the rhythms of the seasons and the constant changes in the natural world.

Many Japanese traditions and festivals
are rooted in nature. In spring, we have
hanami, or flower-viewing, when we hold
parties beneath the cherry blossom in
the brief period while it is flowering.

Some of these trees we come to know
as well as we do people. There is the
famous weeping cherry tree of Tanoue
Kannon-doh, estimated to be several
hundred years old, inside the grounds
of the Tanoue Kannon-doh temple on
the road to Okukiso lake. And the cherry
blossom tree of Suge no Jyuo-doha,
whose large branches spread out across
the village road and over the temple. The
Suge no Jyuo-doha tree is the earliest to
bloom and puts on a spectacular display
of rose-pink flowers up to the sky.

In the autumn, we have tsukimi, or moon-viewing, when we gather together to honour the autumn moon. The ritual is said to have started with the Japanese upper classes, who would recite poetry under the full moon on the fifteenth day of the eighth lunar month, when the moon is at its brightest and most beautiful, and sail in boats so that they could admire its reflection on the surface of the water. Castles were built with turrets specially designed for moon-viewing. For tsukimi, it is traditional to gather with your friends and family where you can see the moon clearly and decorate the place with autumn flowers and pampas grass, which is at its tallest at that time of year.

Never have we been so far from
merging with the natural world and so
divorced from nature. Seventy-eight per
cent of Japanese now live in the city,
most of us in Tokyo, Osaka and Nagoya.
Japan ranks highest in the world for
population density and has become
well known for its extremely crowded
daily life. Pavements are jammed with
pedestrians and bicycles, and there are
rules and routines everywhere to help us
stay out of each other's way.

Eleven million passengers ride the
subway in Tokyo, which is packed to the
brim from first light to late morning
and again on the return commute. We
call this *tsukin jigoku*, or commuter hell.
White-gloved *oshiya*, or pushers, cram
passengers into carriages that were
designed to hold only half as many
people. Commuters have become deft
at performing a dance called the Tokyo
pirouette, in which they squeeze skilfully
into a carriage and find a place to
stand without making eye contact with
anybody else. The average commuter will
spend three and a half years of their life
on the underground train, somewhere
there is not even enough space to read.

And when they miss their train home, they will spend the night in a capsule hotel, once again packed like a sardine in a unit just big enough to lie down in and watch television. Some capsule hotels have as many as seven hundred capsules, or pods.

And, in addition to commuter hell, there is also the phenomenon known as *karoshi*, or death from overwork. In 2016, the Ministry of Health, Labour and Welfare released a Cabinet-endorsed white paper on the extent of working overtime in Japan. Almost 23 per cent of companies said their employees worked more than eighty hours of overtime a month. Of those companies, 11.9 per cent said some employees worked more than a hundred hours of extra time a month. In 2014, a law designed to prevent *karoshi* came into effect, and some companies now compel their employees to take some days off every six months, and turn the lights off at 10 p.m.to encourage them to go home. Nevertheless, about two hundred people die each year from heart attacks, strokes and other *karoshi* events, according to official data.

Why is forest-bathing necessary?

Of course, it is not just in Japan that people have migrated to the city. Across the world, more of us live in a city than do not. Since the year 2000, we have officially become an urban species. The urban population worldwide grew from just 746 million in 1950 to 3.9 billion in 2014, according to the United Nations Population Division. By 2050, 75 per cent of the world's projected 9 billion population will live in cities.

We are also, increasingly, an indoor species. According to the US Environmental Protection Agency, the average American now spends 93 per cent of their time indoors, of which 6 per cent is spent in cars. That makes only one half of one day spent outdoors in a week. Europeans fare no better, spending around 90 per cent of their time indoors.

By 2050, 75 per cent of the world's projected 9 billion population will live in cities.

And what are we doing indoors?
Yes, that's right. We are looking at our
screens. Recent studies have found
that people in the US spend as much
as ten hours and thirty-nine minutes a
day consuming media. A study by the
UK communications regulator Ofcom
shows that people in Britain spend an
average of eight hours and forty-one
minutes a day on their devices, which
is more time than the average person
spends asleep.

And the more time we spend with
new technology, the more likely we
are to suffer because of it. In 1984,
the word 'technostress' was coined to
describe unhealthy behaviour around
new technology. Technostress can arise
from all manner of everyday usage,
like checking your phone constantly,
compulsively sharing updates and
feeling that you need to be continually
connected. Symptoms run from
anxiety, headaches, depression,
mental fatigue, eye and neck strain to
insomnia, frustration, irritability and
loss of temper.

Cities are wonderful places. I love living in Tokyo. Cities are full of excitement, innovation and energy. But living in a city is stressful. And the more we live in them, the more stress we have. The more stress we have, the sicker we get. We have more heart attacks, strokes and cancer. And we have more mental illness, more addictions, loneliness, depression and panic attacks. And, of course, the more stress we have, the more expensive our health care becomes. Anxiety and depression cost the EU about 170 billion euros a year. They cost America $210 billion.

The World Health Organization (WHO) calls stress the health epidemic of the twenty-first century. And finding ways to manage stress — not just for our own health but for the health of our communities, at home and in the workplace — is the most significant health challenge of the future.

The good news is that even a small amount of time in nature can have an impact on our health. A two-hour forest bath will help you to unplug from technology and slow down. It will bring you into the present moment and de-stress and relax you. When you connect to nature through all five of your senses, you begin to draw on the vast array of benefits the natural world provides. There is now a wealth of data that proves that shinrin-yoku can:

- Reduce blood pressure

- Lower stress

- Improve cardiovascular and metabolic health

- Lower blood-sugar levels

- Improve concentration and memory

- Lift depression

- Improve pain thresholds

- Improve energy

- Boost the immune system with an increase in the count of the body's natural killer (NK) cells (see p. 83)

- Increase anti-cancer protein production

- Help you to lose weight

How did this become shinrin-yoku?

In Japan, a national health programme for forest-bathing began to be introduced in 1982. The forest chosen for these early, experimental days of shinrin-yoku was the Akasawa forest in Nagano prefecture, on the old Nakasendo Road, also known as the Samurai Trail. Akasawa is regarded as one of the three most beautiful forests in Japan, with emerald-green rivers fed by the snowmelt waters from Mount Ontake in the west and, in the east, from Mount Kiso-komagatake, the highest peak in the central Alps. In the forest, towering groves of Japanese cypresses, or *hinoki*, stand thirty-five metres tall. They are beautiful trees with dark red trunks of peeling bark and deep-green needles on graceful branches.

The Akasawa forest was the first designated shinrin-yoku site

The wood of the cypress is a beautiful golden colour and has a wonderful scent of lemon and smoke. The slow growth of the trees due to the cold weather means that Japanese cypress is stronger than any other wood and, as far back as the eighth century, it has been used for making statues and Buddhas and in the building of samurai castles. The most prestigious use of timber from the Akasawa forest is in the Ise Shrine, Japan's most important Shinto shrine. Each of its sixty-five structures has to be rebuilt from scratch every twenty years – a symbol of religious renewal that uses wood from as many as ten thousand trees.

The Japanese cypress is recognizable by its dark red bark

During the Edo period, the ruling samurai class protected the trees that grew in the Kiso valley. They were only to be cut for the houses and temples of the powerful families. The rule of one head for one tree was brought in – which meant, as you have no doubt correctly guessed, that if you cut down a tree, your head would be cut off. The five types of trees that were protected have come to be known as the Kiso Goboku, or the Five Sacred Trees of Kiso. They are:

- *Hinoki* cypress (*Chamaecyparis obtusa*)

- *Sawara* cypress (*Chamaecyparis pisifera*)

- *Nezuko* cypress (*Thuja standishii*)

- *Asunaro* cypress (*Thujopsis dolabrata*)

- *Koyamaki*, or Japanese umbrella pine (*Sciadopitys verticillata*)

The Ise Shrine is dedicated to Amaterasu, goddess of the sun

Akasawa is also home to one of Japan's favourite legends, the story of the Japanese Rip Van Winkle, Urashima Tarō. The story goes like this. Once upon a time, a simple fisherman named Urashima Tarō went down to the sea to fish. The sea was rough and he couldn't venture out, but he saw three boys tormenting a turtle that had been washed up on to the shore. Urashima Tarō saved the turtle and released it into the ocean. A little while later, when he was out fishing, the turtle came to him. The turtle was so grateful that he offered to take Urashima Tarō on his back to the underwater Dragon Palace. Thinking it would be an adventure, Tarō went. But after a few days he began to miss his mother and father and wanted to go home. As a parting gift, the sea princess gave him a mysterious casket, the Tamatebako, and told him he must never open it.

When he returned home, everything had
changed and his mother and father were
gone. So Urashima Tarō began to travel.
He wandered through Japan until he
came to the Nezame-no-toko gorge in
the Akasawa forest, where the emerald-
green water of the Kiso river cuts its way
through the rock. Here, he decided to
stay. Then, one day, he remembered the
casket and opened it. A cloud of purple
smoke arose from it and Tarō was turned
into a white-haired old man. He thought
he had been in the underwater palace
only a few days, but in fact he had been
there for hundreds of years. When he
opened the casket, all the time that he
had been gone was unleashed. 'Nezame-
no-toko' means 'Bed of Awakening',
because this is where Urashima Tarō
woke from his 300-year-long sleep.

The forest is now known as the Akasawa National Recreation Forest, or Akasawa-shizen-kyūyō-rin. Kyū means 'rest' or 'break', so, in translation, it is literally a 'rest forest'. In 2001, it was selected as one of the hundred most fragrant forests in Japan. It also has four wonderfully distinct seasons. Spring starts in early April when the cherry blossom begins to appear and the river fills with the meltwaters from the snowfields of Mount Ontake and Mount Kiso-komagatake. The summer is hot, with a beautiful cool breeze blowing over the rocks of the river. October brings a cold wind and lovely autumn colours. When winter arrives, the mountains are often covered with snow.

The river which runs through the Atera valley from Mount Ontake is known for its pristine water and many beautiful waterfalls

So Akasawa has long been known as a place of great beauty and mystery. However, when we began our research there in 1982, there was still a lot to discover about the beneficial properties of trees. Many experiments and much research had to be done before we had scientific evidence to prove what we instinctively felt to be true. In this book, I will take you on a journey and we will discover not only what we have learned about trees but also how to tap into their power. And we will see that, wherever in the world there are trees, we are happier and healthier.

The Akasawa forest was the first designated shinrin-yoku site

The eight walking paths of Akasawa

The *Akasawa* Natural Recreational Forest was designated a forest-therapy base by the Forest Therapy Study Group of Japan in 2006.

There are eight shinrin-yoku trails in the forest, so you can choose a course suited to your level of fitness and to the amount of time you have to spend.

1. **Fureai (Friendship) Trail** (2.8km there and back). This is a paved trail with wooden bridges, so it is suitable for wheelchair users and people who are less steady on their feet. The trail follows the mountain stream gently uphill, and comes back the same way, downhill.

2. **Komadori (Robin) Circuit** (2.7km). This trail takes you past the Ise Shrine sacred tree-felling site and a mountain-stream rest area that is popular with picnickers. You will also pass the giant hinoki cypress and the giant sawara cypress, the two largest trees in the forest. You can branch off this course to join other forest trails.

3. **Mukaiyama Circuit** (2km). This trail
   runs alongside the intertwined 'running
   roots' of cypress trees and through a mass
   of magnolia trees. In mid-June, you can
   enjoy the scent of the flowers as they come
   into bloom. From this trail you can also
   see Mount Kiso-komagutake and Mount
   Norikura in the distance.

4. **Nakadachi Circuit** (2.1km). This trail
   climbs up to the Nakadachi viewpoint,
   taking you through hinoki forest and past
   rare sawara and hiba cypresses.

5. **Tsumetazawa Circuit** (3.3km). This
   course takes you deeper into the forest
   than any of the other trails. At the highest
   part of the trail, the hinoki cypress trees
   are among the tallest trees in the forest.
   Flowers bloom on the forest floor at the
   end of April, so it looks like 'stars are
   scattered at our feet'.

6. **Kami-Akasawa Circuit** (2.2km). There
   are many changes in the landscape along
   this route, which takes you through both
   natural and plantation forests and past
   deciduous broadleaf trees as well as the
   famous evergreens. At the top of the trail,
   there are beautiful views of Mount Ontake.

7. **Keiryu (Mountain Stream) Circuit**
(1.5km). The trickling sound of running
water accompanies you on this course. Here,
you will feel the moisture in the air from
the stream and a refreshing breeze. This is
the shortest course, but it connects to the
Himemiya Bridge, which will take you on
further if you want to enjoy more of the
mountain stream.

8. **Keiryu (Mountain Stream) Circuit**,
Himemiya Route (3.5km one way). This
is a beautiful trail to follow to enjoy the
different seasons. In the spring, there are
banks of flowering rhododendrons, and in
the autumn the trees turn bright shades
of orange.

In addition to the trails, there is also a therapy
centre with a consultation room for forest
medicine. As well as being the birthplace of
forest-bathing, Akasawa was the first forest
base to have medical staff on site. Every
Thursday from May to October, you can have a
consultation among the trees. Since 2007, Kiso
Hospital has offered forest-therapy check-ups:
you receive a health check at the hospital and
then, on the doctor's advice, go for shinrin-
yoku. A hundred thousand people now visit
this forest every year.

1.

From a Feeling to a Science

Forests are an amazing resource. They give us everything we rely on in order to exist. They produce oxygen, cleanse the air we breathe and purify our water. They stop flooding rivers and streams and the erosion of mountains and hills. They provide us with food, clothing and shelter, and with the materials we need for furniture and tools. In addition to this, forests have always helped us to heal our wounds and to cure our diseases. And, from time immemorial, they have relieved us of our worries, eased our troubled minds, restored and refreshed us. Until recently, however, there was little scientific evidence to support what we have always known innately about the healing power of the forest.

When people started to practise
shinrin-yoku, in the early 1980s,
it was based only on common
sense and the intuitive idea
that being in the beautiful
green forests of Japan would
be good for us. The term was
invented in 1982 by the then
Director General of the Agency
of Agriculture, Forestry and
Fisheries of Japan, Tomohide
Akiyama, who stated that the
people of Japan were in need
of healing through nature. The
idea was also part of a campaign
to protect the forests. If people
were encouraged to visit forests
for their health, they would be
more likely to want to protect
and look after them.

In 1990, a preliminary research group
went to Yakushima, a small, round
island seventeen miles in diameter off
southern Japan. Yakushima contains
some of Japan's most pristine forests,
both subtropical and alpine, and
there are waterfalls and hot springs.
Thousands of different species of
plants and hundreds of types of moss
paint the forest a luminous, glowing
green. The island has one of the wettest
climates in the world. It is said to rain
there for thirty-five days a month!
Deer and monkeys roam free and with
its dripping jungle of moss-covered
sugi trees – Yakusugi – the forest has
a mysterious, otherworldly beauty. It
looks like it might have looked at the
beginning of time.

LEFT: Yakushima island contains
some of Japan's most pristine forests

BELOW: The moss-covered Jomon
Cedar is the biggest sugi tree on
Yakushima

What would the effect of walking on Yakushima be? How would people feel doing shinrin-yoku in the forest there?

In fact, I already knew this, from personal experience. I spent a week camping with my friends in that mysterious, glowing, green forest in 1988, when I was a student. I went during Golden Week – a holiday in Japan which includes Greenery Day, a day on which we commune with nature and are thankful for all its bounty and beauty. I didn't realize it then, of course, but it now seems very appropriate! It was while I was on Yakushima during Golden Week that I became convinced that forest-bathing was absolutely essential to human health. That fascinating, inspiring visit was to have an important impact on the whole direction of my life and my future research.

That preliminary research trip in 1990 was more a speculative investigation than a scientific inquiry. It was filmed by Japanese television and showed that walking in the forest was associated with improved mood and increased energy. It was still a way off, but we were now at least on the road to understanding the feeling of health and wellness that being in the forest gives us.

It was not until 2004 that scientific investigation of the link between forests and human health began in earnest. Together with various government agencies and academic organizations in Japan – and still feeling inspired by my experiences on Yakushima – I helped found the Forest Therapy Study Group, with the express aim of discovering what it is about trees that makes us feel so much better. The following year, I set off for Iiyama city, in the mountainous north-western corner of Nagano Prefecture, taking twelve healthy middle-aged businessmen from Tokyo with me for a three-day scientific forest-bathing trip.

The forests of Iiyama are some of the
most beautiful and unspoilt in Japan.
With the giant beech trees of Mount
Nahekura and the snowmelt waters of
the Chikumagawa (also known as the
Shinanogawa), the country's longest
river, the landscape is quintessentially
Japanese. This is the romantic setting of
traditional folk songs such as 'Oborozukiyo'
(or 'Moonlit Night'), which tells of a
beautiful spring night in the countryside,
and 'Furusato'. Furusato means 'old home'
or 'home town' and the composer of the
song grew up in Nagano, near the forests
of Iiyama. The song is full of yearning for
the mountains and fields of his boyhood
home. What better place for the world's
first forest-bathing experiment!

It was in Iiyama that we first scientifically
proved that forest-bathing can:

• Boost the immune system

• Increase energy

• Decrease anxiety, depression and anger

• Reduce stress and bring about a state
  of relaxation

Measuring Stress

The nervous system is made up of the sympathetic system (also known as the 'fight or flight' part), and the parasympathetic system (or the 'rest and recover' part). Let's say you are walking along the street and a sabre-toothed tiger jumps out at you: your fight-or-flight responses will start up. Your heart will beat faster, your blood pressure will increase and your digestion will slow down.

When you are relaxing, by going for a forest bath for example, the opposite happens. Your blood pressure decreases, your pulse rate slows and the rate of digestion can speed up. And, as well as increasing blood pressure and heart rate, stress also throws the two parts of the nervous system out of balance. It strengthens the fight-or-flight part and suppresses the rest-and-recover part, meaning we are constantly on high alert.

We all know what it feels like to have
these parts of our system out of balance
– and it isn't pleasant! I feel it when I
have been on night duty in my hospital,
or am having building work done in my
apartment. Or when I have to work on
Sunday and don't have time for a forest
bath.

Another good way to tell if something
is stressful is to measure cortisol levels.
Cortisol is a 'stress hormone': we release
it when we are anxious or under stress.
As with our heart rate, cortisol levels are,
generally, self-regulating. Stress hormones
are released to help us deal with a threat
or a stressful event – that sabre-toothed
tiger again, perhaps, or just the next-door
neighbour's dog barking loudly. Once the
stressful event is over, hormone levels
return to normal, your heart stops beating
so fast and you can relax again.

If you commuted into work today, you
will have been under stress – navigating
traffic, dealing with crowded trains,
waiting in the rain for a bus that never
comes. And your body will have released

cortisol to deal with it. The problem with our busy city lives, however, is that the stressful events keep piling up. There will be emails to answer, co-workers demanding attention, a deadline looming, the shopping to get done, the bills to be paid. And our cortisol levels remain always slightly raised.

When cortisol is released constantly, it can disrupt all our body's processes, and people who produce chronically high levels of cortisol are at increased risk of numerous health problems.

The **good news** is that my studies, and those of my fellow researchers, have now proved that forest-bathing:

- Lowers the stress hormones cortisol and adrenaline

- Suppresses the sympathetic or 'fight or flight' system

- Enhances the parasympathetic or 'rest and recover' system

- Lowers blood pressure and increases heart-rate variability

Based on the results of that forest-bathing study in April 2006, Iiyama became the first location in Japan to receive forest-therapy certification. The 'green healing' power of Iiyama's forests had been scientifically demonstrated. There are now sixty-two certified forest-therapy bases in Japan, all of which have been proved to have particular healthful properties, and between 2.5 and 5 million people now walk the forest trails every year. Shinrin-yoku has become standard practice, a way in which Japanese people can manage their stress and look after their health.

We have now conducted numerous studies and collected a huge mass of data from hundreds of people on the impact of forest-bathing on various aspects of human health. Here are a few of our findings . . .

Between 2.5 and 5 million people now walk the forest trails every year.

Forest-bathing can help you sleep

Not being able to sleep is a well-known side effect of stress. It won't surprise you to learn that, in Japan, 30–40 per cent of working-age men say they can't sleep because of stress, and 40 per cent say that they sleep less than six hours a night. Doctors typically recommend eight hours. Good-quality and adequate sleep is vital for our health and well-being. It helps our brains to work properly, it balances our hormones and is essential for the proper functioning of our immune system. Sleep deficiency is linked to numerous health problems, including increased risk of heart disease, kidney disease, high blood pressure, diabetes and stroke.

I wanted to investigate whether shinrin-yoku could improve sleep patterns, so I also studied the effect of forest-bathing on sleep in Iiyama city with the same twelve middle-aged male office workers from Tokyo.

The participants took two-hour walks in the morning and afternoon in different forests. They walked around 2.5km in two hours – roughly the same distance they would walk on a normal working day. I measured their sleep activity with a sleep polygraph and an accelerometer – a counter you wear on your wrist like a watch which judges the number of physical movements you make – before, during and after the trip. Fewer than forty body movements in a minute indicates that a person is asleep.

Before the forest-bathing trip, these men had an average sleep time of 383 minutes. On the nights during the trip, this rose to 452 minutes. And on the night after the trip, it was 410 minutes. In other words, there was a significant increase in sleep time during the forest-bathing trip, proving that you sleep better when you spend time in a forest, even when you don't significantly increase the amount of physical activity you do.

Another sleep study reported by other researchers looked at how forest-bathing improved sleep for a group of people who suffered from sleep complaints of one kind or another, from insomnia and difficulty falling asleep or staying asleep to waking up early in the morning. The group walked for two hours in Ryukoku forest in the western part of Honshu. Sleep was measured the night before and the night after. Comparisons were made between the two nights and between people who walked in the morning and in the afternoon.

Here are some of the findings:

- The average sleep time of participants after a two-hour forest walk increased by 15 per cent, or fifty-four minutes

- Participants were significantly less anxious after a two-hour walk in the forest

- Quality of sleep was better after forest-bathing

- Afternoon walks improved the quality of sleep more than morning walks

Forest-bathing can improve your mood

It is not a secret that high levels of stress are directly linked to anger and irritability. Our modern-day lives are exhausting. We are pulled in so many different directions at once. So, I wonder how you start the day after a night of not quite enough sleep. Is it standing at the kitchen counter with a cup of coffee? Is it rushing to catch a train or to get the children to school? Are there a million and one things you have to do as soon as you get into work, which ought to have been done yesterday? And how does that make you feel? Happy and relaxed, full of energy and enthusiasm for life? No, I thought not.

It probably won't surprise you by now to learn that forest-bathing can help here, too. One of the ways we measure the impact of forest-bathing on mood is through the POMS (Profile of Mood States) test. Participants are given a list of sixty-five emotions and asked to rate the extent to which they are currently experiencing each one on a scale ranging from 'not at all' to 'extremely'. The questionnaire is taken twice — before and after a forest-bathing trip.

Some of the emotions on the list are:

Confusion

Sadness

Terror

Guilt

Vigour

Exhaustion

In my studies using the POMS test, I took two groups of men and women on a forest-bathing trip for three days and two nights. I also took two groups of men and women for a two-hour walk in the forest. And just to make sure the effects weren't due merely to the exercise, I also took them on a walk in downtown Tokyo, where there are no trees. The results show that:

- Although walking anywhere (in an urban or a forest setting) reduces the scores for anxiety, depression, anger and confusion, **it is ONLY walking in forest environments that has a positive effect on vigour and fatigue**

- A two-hour trip to the forest had a similar effect on POMS scores as longer excursions, so the good news is **you don't have to spend a lot of time in the forest**. Two hours is enough

- Women's moods seem to be affected more by forest-bathing than men's

These are, of course, subjective scores, but objective data backs them up. The levels of measurable stress hormones in women fell after forest-bathing, which supports the improvement in mood they recorded on their POMS questionnaires.

At the back of this book, you will find a POMS questionnaire for you to use on your forest-bathing trip so you can see the improvement in mood for yourself.

Every Monday when I take my students for shinrin-yoku in the city parks in Tokyo, I make them fill in the POMS questionnaire before we set off and then again when we come back so they can measure the improvement in their moods and see for themselves the powerful effect of forest-bathing.

Lisa's story

In my third year at medical school, I went forest-bathing every Monday as part of my studies. I had heard about shinrin-yoku before, but I didn't know it was something that could be scientifically studied. I grew up in the city and spent very little time in nature. But after I had participated in shinrin-yoku research, I began to need time in nature to relax, and now I always do shinrin-yoku when I have been studying hard. I can feel the seasons by seeing the colours of the leaves and the flowers.

Before I did shinrin-yoku, I didn't really believe that forest-bathing could make me feel better. I was very surprised to see how effective it was. After I do forest-bathing, I feel tired, but I also feel good and relaxed. The feeling lasts all night. My hobby is classical ballet and I have been taking lessons since I was three years old, so ballet dancing helps me deal with stress. But when I don't have time for lessons, shinrin-yoku helps me.

The Showa Memorial Park is just outside Tokyo

Yuya's story

My favourite park to go to for shinrin-yoku is Shinjuku Gyoen. This is right in the middle of Tokyo and was designed so that people could appreciate all the beauty of the Japanese landscape there. I like forest-bathing. I often go to a park on my own, and it always makes me feel refreshed. Forest-bathing is similar to doing sport in the way it can relieve stress. To begin with, I found it difficult to believe in the effect forest-bathing could have, but now I have experienced it for myself I know how powerful it can be. Plus, there is statistical evidence that proves it helps!

Shinjuku Gyoen National Garden is located right in the heart of Tokyo

Forest-bathing boosts the immune system

So, forest-bathing can help you sleep and it can put you in a better mood, making you less aggressive and hostile and generally less grumpy all round. It lowers your heart rate and your blood pressure and improves your cardiovascular and metabolic health. And, most importantly, it can boost your immune system.

It is well known that the immune system plays an important part in building our defences against bacteria, viruses and tumours. It is also well known that stress inhibits immune function. If your immune system is suppressed, you are more likely to be ill; stressed people are frequently ill.

One of the ways we test the health of the immune system is by looking at the activity of our natural killer (NK) cells. Natural killer cells are a type of white blood cell and are so called because they can attack and kill unwanted cells, for example, those infected with a virus, or tumour cells. They do this with the help of anti-cancer proteins: perforin, granulysin and granzymes. These proteins drill holes in cell membranes and this causes the target cells to die. People with higher NK activity show a lower incidence of diseases such as cancer.

In the first forest-bathing study I undertook in Iiyama, I found that after three days and two nights in the forest:

- NK cell activity went up from 17.3 per cent to 26.5 per cent – a 53.2 per cent increase

- NK cell numbers went up from 440 to 661 – a 50 per cent increase

- The presence of anti-cancer protein granulysin was up by 48 per cent, granzyme A by 39 per cent, granzyme B by 33 per cent, and perforin by 28 per cent

I also wanted to know how long the increased natural killer activity would last, so the following year I did another three days and two nights forest-bathing research trip, this time in three different forests around Agematsu town, in Nagano prefecture, the birth-place of shinrin-yoku. This area is full of hinoki trees and has some of the most beautiful, fragrant forests in Japan. There are almost no mosquitoes in the forests here because of the scent from these Japanese cypress trees. Maybe you don't believe me, but it's true!

The Kiso river flows through Agematsu town

I took measurements on a normal working day before the trip and again one, two, seven and thirty days after the trip was over. The results showed that natural killer activity and the number of natural killer cells were significantly increased after forest-bathing and that this effect lasted not just for seven days but for as long as thirty days.

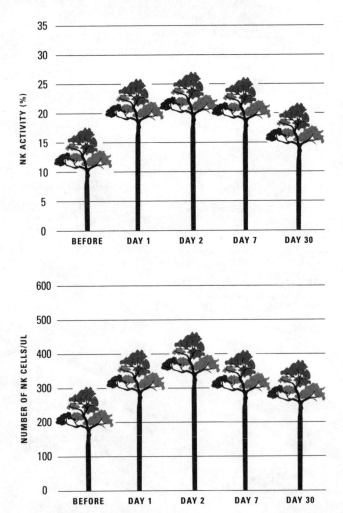

Hence, a forest-bathing trip once a month is enough to maintain a high level of natural killer cell activity.

These studies suggested that forests may have anti-cancer effects through this enhancement of natural killer cell activity. If you can raise your NK cell activity just by going for a walk in nature, what would be the effect if you lived near trees all the time? How great could the anti-cancer effects be if you lived in a green place?

So I set out to look at the relationship between forest coverage in Japan and deaths from different kinds of cancer – and I found that people who live in areas with fewer trees not only have significantly higher levels of stress, they also have higher mortality rates than people who live where there is a good density of trees.

The power of trees

What is it about trees that has this effect? How exactly do trees do this?

I knew that our five senses played a crucial role in forest-bathing's healing effects – the sights, sounds, smells, tastes and feel of the forest all have a powerful impact on our well-being. Of all our senses, sense of smell is most primal. Could it be that breathing in the forest's natural aromatherapy – the plant chemicals known as phytoncides – is what was providing this huge boost to the immune system?

It took a long time to discover the answer to this. But let me explain first what a phytoncide is.

As well as having a higher
concentration of oxygen, the air in
the forest is also full of phytoncides.
Phytoncides are the natural oils
within a plant and are part of a
tree's defence system. Trees release
phytoncides to protect them from
bacteria, insects and fungi. *Phyton* is
Greek for 'plant', and *cide* is 'to kill'.
Phytoncides are also part of the
communication pathway between
trees: the way trees talk to each other.
The concentration of phytoncides in
the air depends on the temperature
and other changes that take place
throughout the year. The warmer it is,
the more phytoncides there are in the
air. The concentration of phytoncides
is at its highest at temperatures of
around 30 degrees Celsius.

Phytoncides vary from tree species
to tree species and have very specific
scents. One of the most familiar smells
in Japan is the scent of the Japanese
hinoki cypress, *Chamaecyparis obtusa*. It is a
nostalgic and meaningful smell for many
Japanese because this is the wood we
use to build our shrines, our houses –
and even our baths.

Evergreens like pine trees, cedars, spruces and conifers are the largest producers of phytoncides. We will look more at what the forest smells like in the next chapter. For now, it will be enough to explain that the main components of phytoncides are terpenes, and these are what you can smell when you do shinrin-yoku in the forest. The major terpenes are:

D-limonene – which smells, you guessed it, lemony

Alpha-pinene – this is the most common terpene in nature and has a very fresh, piney scent

Beta-pinene – smells more herby, like basil or dill

Camphene – which has a turpentiney, resinous smell

Alpha-pinene, beta-pinene and D-limonene were among the phytoncides measured in the air in the forests when I conducted the studies on mood with the POMS questionnaire. Exposure to essential oils was already known to lift depression and help with anxiety, so it seemed clear that the phytoncides in the air must be part of what was making my forest-bathers feel so much better and more relaxed. But there had been no investigation into the effect of phytoncides on natural killer cell function. So I decided to test them.

In my first experiment, I incubated human natural killer cells with phytoncides for five to seven days. The wood essential oils I used were:

Chamaecyparis leaf oil (hinoki)

Chamaecyparis stem oil (hinoki)

Cryptomeria stem oil (Japanese cedar)

Hiba stem oil (white cedar)

Chamaecyparis taiwanensis stem oil

Alpha-pinene, 1.8-cineol and D-limonene

At the end of five to seven days' incubation, the results showed that both the NK cell activity and the presence of the anti-cancer proteins perforin, granzyme A and granulysin had increased.

The next thing to do was to test the
effect of phytoncides on immune
function in people. This time, I took
twelve healthy middle-aged men
to stay at a hotel in Tokyo for three
nights, and I diffused *hinoki* stem oil
into their rooms while they slept.

ABOVE AND OVERLEAF:
The smell from the *hinoki* tree
is my favourite phytoncide
smell; here it is in full bloom

Hinoki is my favourite phytoncide smell.
It is a very nostalgic scent for me,
reminding me of many happy times. I
gave the men a choice of different wood
essential oils, but they all preferred
hinoki – like me! During the winter, I
diffuse hinoki stem oil with a humidifier
in my room every day, for my health.
During the summer, I put a bottle of
hinoki oil in my room to produce the
aromatic smell.

But back to the experiment . . . The men
all went to bed at 11 p.m. and worked
as usual during the day. To ensure that
there were no extraneous factors, we
limited physical activity during the
study to the distance walked on an
average working day. The concentration
of phytoncides in the air in the hotel
bedrooms was also measured.

Results showed that exposure to phytoncides:

- Significantly increased the numbers of NK cells and NK activity, as well as enhancing the activity of the anti-cancer proteins

- Significantly decreased the levels of stress hormones

- Increased the hours of sleep

- Decreased the scores for tension/ anxiety, anger/hostility and fatigue/ confusion.

Other researchers have shown that phytoncides can:

- Stimulate a pleasant mood

- Significantly lower blood pressure and heart rate

- Increase heart-rate variability

- Suppress sympathetic nervous activity and increase parasympathetic nervous activity, bringing your nervous system into balance and making you feel comfortable and relaxed

In fact, one study, at the Department of Psychiatry at Mie University in Japan, has shown that the citrus fragrance of the phytoncide D-limonene is more effective than antidepressants for lifting mood and ensuring emotional well-being in patients with mental-health disorders.

One example of the power of essential oils to reduce stress was shown by two nurses who worked in the emergency department at Vanderbilt University Medical Center. They and their co-workers often experienced very high levels of stress and fatigue. Both the nurses had used essential oils at home to manage their stress and exhaustion and wondered what the effect would be if they could diffuse the oils throughout the department. A wellness committee was set up to approve the study and to make sure the experiment complied with hospital regulations, and that it would not interfere with the standard of care that patients expected.

The results showed the enormous
impact that diffusing oils can have on a
stressful working environment. Before
the use of essential oils, 41 per cent of
staff reported that they felt work-related
stress very often. After the oils were
diffused in the department, this dropped
to 3 per cent. Before the use of essential
oils, 13 per cent of staff reported feeling
well equipped to handle stressful
situations at work. Afterwards, this rose
to 58 per cent. Perceived energy levels
increased from 33 per cent to 77 per
cent. At the end of the study, 84 per cent
of staff 'strongly agreed' that diffusing
essential oils contributed to a more
positive work environment.

The wellness committee mission
statement listed sixty-eight hospitals
and other institutions throughout the
US that already employed essential oils,
and noted that the Harris Methodist
Fort Worth Hospital in Texas uses thirty-
three different types of essential oils,
dispensed from their own pharmacy.

The nurses said, 'Imagine the possibilities if essential oils can have this kind of impact on the working environment, even changing the perception of one's stress and energy levels.'

Pharmaceutical companies can only dream of creating a pill that has this sort of power!

Why don't you try diffusing your favourite essential oils at home and see what effects they have? You may be amazed. I will show you how to do it later in the book (page 232).

Microbes

There is also a substance in soil that we breathe in when we walk in the forest and which makes us feel happier. This is a common and harmless bacteria, *Mycobacterium vaccae*.

The benefits of *Mycobacterium vaccae* were discovered almost by accident by Dr Mary O'Brien, an oncologist at the Royal Marsden Hospital, London. Dr O'Brien was conducting an experiment to see if injecting patients with lung cancer with M. *vaccae* would boost their immune systems and help them fight the disease. Her experiment found no proof that it did, but she did make an unexpected discovery: an injection of the bacteria 'significantly improved patient quality of life'. Her patients reported feeling more positive and having higher energy levels and better cognitive functioning.

A few years later, scientists at Bristol University (UK) injected M. *vaccae* into mice. They were trying to find out why, when people become sick, they often become depressed. When they injected the mice, they found that the mice behaved as though they were on antidepressants. This was very interesting in itself, but the scientists also discovered something else. The neurons that were

activated were those associated with the immune system, which suggested that there is a close connection between the immune system and our emotions. In other words, the soil stimulates the immune system, and a boosted immune system makes us feel happy. Every time you dig in your garden or eat a vegetable plucked from the ground, you will be ingesting M. *vaccae* and giving yourself this boost.

More evidence that being in the forest atmosphere and using all your senses is good for your health, and a very good reason for getting your hands dirty while you are there!

A boosted immune system makes us feel happy.

Trees help us think more clearly,
be more creative, and make us nicer
and more generous.

So what about our emotional health
in the forest, that improvement in
our mental well-being that we feel so
immediately when we are in nature?
Plenty of research substantiates what
leaders, poets and philosophers have
known since the days of Aristotle:
walking in the forest clears our minds
and helps us to think.

Walking in
the forest
clears our
minds, and
helps us
to think.

One study undertaken by the University of Michigan that looked at the effects on memory and attention when we engage with nature found that people could remember 20 per cent more after they had been for a walk where there are trees than when they had walked through busy city streets, no matter what the weather (though the participants enjoyed the walks more when it wasn't cold!).

Walking in nature has also been shown by researchers at Stanford University to help us stop brooding on our problems. This study was conducted on a group of students who each took a series of memory tests and mood assessments before setting off for a walk. One half of the students went to a leafy, green part of the university campus, the other half walked along a busy road with heavy traffic. They took another set of tests when they came back.

The results showed that not only does walking in nature alleviate feelings of anxiety and other negative emotions, but it also increases positive thoughts. In other words, walking in nature can help us to change the way we think about things and see them in a better light.

Nature also has the power to help us solve problems and to break through creative blocks. Research at the universities of Utah and Kansas looked at the effect on creative reasoning skills of being immersed in nature for a number of days. The researchers concluded that there 'is a real, measurable cognitive advantage to be realized if we spend time truly immersed in a natural setting', and found that spending time in nature can boost problem-solving ability and creativity by 50 per cent.

Is it any wonder that Buddha found enlightenment sitting under a tree?

Spending time in nature can boost problem-solving ability and creativity by 50 per cent.

Anna's story

I have suffered from writer's block on
and off for many years. Just at the point
at which I think I will never be able to get
down another word and am in despair, I
take myself off to the countryside to walk
in nature. I have a place I always go to. The
air there is very special and it is the first
thing I notice. It's full of wild thyme and
rosemary, and often I just stand still and
breathe. The smell is especially beautiful
after there has been a gentle rain. Then
I start to look around. As my eyes travel
across the landscape, I can almost feel my
brain untangling. I can't tell you how many
times I have got to the countryside after
being bent over my work for weeks, unable
to sort out a problem which just gets
knottier the more I try to work on it, and
solved it. The only solution for me is to be
in nature. Sometimes it is as though the
answer I'm looking for is right there in the
trees and all I had to do was get there.

It might seem obvious that nature can help us to think more positively and clearly, but did you know that nature can also make you more trusting, helpful and caring?

Several studies have shown that, when we connect with nature, we are reminded that we are part of something larger than ourselves. Faced with the awesome vastness of the universe, we can feel flooded with gratitude. We become less selfish and start to think about others. And you don't have to be alone on a mountainside to experience the wondrous splendour of the natural world. Researchers have shown that we become more helpful and caring after watching DVDs of *Planet Earth* and looking at pictures of breathtakingly tall trees.

And even more amazing is the fact that not only do the beautiful and magnificent sights of nature make us feel better, they can actually improve our health. Research has demonstrated that positive emotions of the kind we experience when we look at nature can increase our levels of anti-inflammatory cytokines. These are the proteins that tell the immune system to work harder. And anything that makes our immune system work harder is a boost to our health.

There is no medicine you can take that has such a direct influence on your health as a walk in a beautiful forest.

Soft fascination

One idea for why the natural landscape has such
a powerful effect on us is the theory that we pay
attention differently when we are in nature. The
great nineteenth-century thinker William James
(brother of the novelist Henry James) explained
that there are two ways of paying attention. The first
is 'voluntary', or directed, which is used for tasks
that demand effort and concentration. It is what we
use when we are at work, or driving, or even just
navigating our way along a busy street. All sorts of
things demand our directed attention: shopfronts
and advertising billboards, ticket machines and
traffic lights. Because of this, just a few moments in
a city street can bring on mental fatigue.

The second is 'involuntary', sometimes called 'soft
fascination', which I think is a lovely expression.
Involuntary attention requires no mental effort, it
just comes naturally. This is the kind of attention
we use when we are in nature. In nature, our minds
are captured effortlessly by clouds and sunsets, by
the movement of leaves in the breeze, by waterfalls
and streams, by the sound of the birds or the
whisper of the wind. These soothing sights and
sounds give our mental resources a break. They
allow our minds to wander and to reflect, and so
restore our capacity to think more clearly.

Room with a view

Some of the most important research on how a view of nature can help us to heal has been done by American professor of healthcare design Roger Ulrich. His most famous paper is 'View through a Window May Influence Recovery from Surgery'. As a young researcher in the early 1980s, he collected information on patients who had just had abdominal surgery. He was baffled as to why some patients recovered quickly and were sent home while others took a week or two longer to get better.

As a teenager, Ulrich had suffered long bouts of kidney disease and spent many weeks at home in bed. What helped him through those days of illness was the view of a large pine tree which grew outside his window. He wondered if the difference in the patients' recovery time had anything to do with the view from their windows, some of which were of trees, while others were of a brick wall.

He discovered that patients whose room looked out on to trees recovered more quickly than those whose rooms faced the wall. Those who looked on to the wall needed more medication for pain and spent longer in hospital. They were also more depressed.

In a later study at a Swedish hospital, Ulrich randomly assigned heart-surgery patients in intensive care to a series of 'views', or pictures. The patients who recovered more smoothly, needed less pain medication and suffered less anxiety were those shown photographs of an open, tree-lined stream.

Many studies since then have shown that having a hospital window with a view of nature improves healing. Patients with a 'green' view need less medication and are discharged sooner after surgery than those who don't have a window or whose room looks out on to a wall.

When trees die, people die

One of the biggest 'natural experiments' on the relationship between trees and human health was carried out as a result of the emerald ash borer disease in America.

The emerald ash borer is a small green beetle, and is thought to have come over from China to the US in wooden packing cases. Emerald ash borer disease was first noticed in 2002 in trees in the American Midwest, and spread rapidly when trees infested with the beetle were cut down, mainly for firewood, and transported across the country. There are 7 billion ash trees in America, and emerald ash borer disease could, potentially, kill most of them. Over 100 million trees have died so far.

The most obvious effect of the disease was to turn once-leafy neighbourhoods into treeless areas. Ash trees are a dominant feature of American streets and account for about a quarter of trees in public spaces. Less obviously, the US Forest Service found that, in the places where trees had been affected by the disease, mortality rates were higher — specifically, the rates of death from cardiovascular and respiratory tract disease, which are two of the most common causes of death in America.

One study looking at the relationship between emerald ash borer disease and mortality rates in fifteen counties between 1990 and 2007 equated the deaths of trees from the disease with 15,080 deaths from heart disease and 6,113 deaths from diseases of the lower respiratory system. It also found that the greater the infestation, the greater its effect on human health.

More trees, more happiness

All of this adds to the growing evidence that trees provide major public health benefits. Now that more than half of us live in the city, urban green spaces are more important than ever for our health and well-being – and that includes our psychological and emotional well-being.

More trees means more happiness. One extensive study conducted at the University of Exeter (UK) found that people who live where there are trees and green spaces are less anxious and depressed – and that the positive effects of trees on people's

The positive effect of trees on people's mental well-being last longer than short-term boosts to happiness.

mental well-being last longer than short-term boosts to happiness such as getting a pay rise or getting married. Another study looking at the density of trees and the number of prescriptions issued for antidepressants in London found that residents of the streets with the most trees took out fewer prescriptions than those who lived in areas with few or no trees.

A group of Canadian, American and Australian researchers studying tree density and health in Toronto found that having ten more trees on a city block can make residents feel as good as being given a $10,000 pay rise or being seven years younger. Having eleven more trees on a block lowered cardio-metabolic illnesses, like high blood pressure, diabetes and obesity, comparable to the effects on well-being conferred by being given a $20,000 a year pay rise or being 1.4 years younger.

Trees can make you feel richer and younger!

In other words, trees can make you feel richer and younger!

They can also extend your life. Research in Japan on elderly people has found that people live longer when their homes are within walking distance of a park or green space.

2.

How to Practise Shinrin-Yoku

The forest is like our mother, a sacred place, a gift to us humans from the divine. It is a paradise of healing. Mother Nature fills us with wonder and curiosity and invites us in. She works in harmony with us and with our innate capacity for healing. This is the foundation of forest medicine. In the forest, we begin to reconnect with nature and journey towards health and happiness. The art of forest-bathing is the art of connecting with nature through our senses. All we have to do is accept the invitation. Mother Nature does the rest.

The art of forest-bathing is the art of connecting with nature through our senses.

First, find a spot . . .

Make sure you have left your
phone and camera behind. You
are going to be walking aimlessly
and slowly. You don't need any
devices. Let your body be your
guide. Listen to where it wants to
take you. Follow your nose. And
take your time. It doesn't matter
if you don't get anywhere. You
are not going anywhere. You are
savouring the sounds, smells and
sights of nature and letting the
forest in.

The key to unlocking the power
of the forest is in the five senses.
Let nature enter through your
ears, eyes, nose, mouth, hands
and feet.

Engage your five senses ...

- Listen to the birds singing and the breeze rustling in the leaves of the trees

- Look at the different greens of the trees and the sunlight filtering through the branches

- Smell the fragrance of the forest and breathe in the natural aromatherapy of phytoncides

- Taste the freshness of the air as you take deep breaths

- Place your hands on the trunk of a tree. Dip your fingers or toes in a stream. Lie on the ground

- Drink in the flavour of the forest and release your sense of joy and calm. This is your sixth sense, a state of mind. Now you have connected with nature. You have crossed the bridge to happiness

How to make the most of the forest

When it comes to finding calm and relaxation, there is no one-size-fits-all solution – it differs from person to person. For some, it will be the sound of water flowing over pebbles in a stream or squirrels chattering to each other in the branches. For others, it is the scent of the air, or the sight of the forest bursting into green at the beginning of spring.

It is important to find a place that suits you. If you love the smell of damp soil, you will be most relaxed where the natural landscape provides it. Then the effects of the forest will be more powerful. Maybe you have a place in the countryside that reminds you of your childhood or of happy times in the past. These places will be special to you and your connection with them will be strong.

When looking for a place to go for shinrin-yoku, check what the forest is like beforehand. Is it a forest where you can see the changes of the season, or one that is famous for the sound of trickling water, or for its views of mountains and lakes? Look for a place where you can feel comfortable, somewhere that will fill your heart with joy.

Look for a place where you can feel comfortable, somewhere that will fill your heart with joy.

Find what works best for you

When you have been busy at work all week, it can be hard to slow down. You may have been rushing around so much you no longer know how to stand still. In many forest bases around the world, you will find a guide who can help you to engage your senses while you are in the woods. A guide can help to slow you down, to connect you with nature and let the forest do its therapeutic work. Walking with a guide who is a trained forest therapist can help you feel more comfortable and find the right environment to fit your needs. In one of my favourite forests, Iinan Furusato-no-Mori, the forest-therapy programme includes guided walks. Doctors are on hand to offer general health assessments. When you arrive, you are given a physical health check and a psychological questionnaire. The therapist then works out the best walking plan for you.

But it is just as easy to forest-bathe without a guide. In this book, I am your guide. Here you will find instructions and exercises to help you forest-bathe alone. I will share with you everything I know about shinrin-yoku and teach you how to use your senses to connect with nature and unlock the power that lies within the forest.

There are many different activities you can do in the forest that will help you to relax and to connect with nature. It doesn't matter how fit – or unfit – you are. Shinrin-yoku is suitable for any level of fitness. Here are some of the things people do:

Forest walking You can walk as slowly as you like. Slow walking is recommended for beginners. It is important not to hurry through the forest. You are not going on a hike. Walking slowly will help you to keep your senses open, to notice things and to smell the forest air. Stop every now and then to take in your surroundings and see what else your senses notice.

Yoga It doesn't take long to reap the benefits of a yoga session done outdoors. Focus on relaxing your muscles and your breathing. You can do a few easy poses, or sit comfortably with your legs crossed. Breathe deeply and take in the sights and smells around you. Listen to the sounds of the forest.

Eating in the forest Meals of edible plants are a vital part of the forest-therapy programme in some bases. The countryside surrounding Iinan, for example, is a rich source of medicinal foods and herbs. The forest-base restaurants offer local specialities such as *sasazushi* (sushi on a bamboo leaf) and Tomikura soba noodles, made from the leaves of the *oyamabokuchi* plant (similar to burdock) which are considered a delicacy among soba connoisseurs. (Some forest-therapy bases even teach you how to make them.) Wherever you are, you can forage for wild foods or look for the specialities of the area to take with you on your picnic. There is no better way to taste the flavour of a region than to eat the foods that are grown there.

WARNING: *Be very careful when foraging for wild food. There are plenty of poisonous plants, and they often resemble edible ones. Never eat anything you have picked in the wild that you are not a hundred per cent certain is safe to eat.*

Hot-spring therapy This is for the lucky
people, like the Japanese, who have
natural hot springs in their country.
There are four hot springs, or *onsen*,
in the town of Iinan, with natural
temperatures of around 38 to 40
degrees Celsius. You can bathe in the
waters and listen to the sound of
the river while you gaze out on to
the mountain landscape. The forest
therapists in Furusato-no-mori
recommend bathing in a hot spring
after every forest walk.

Here are some other activities to try:

- T'ai chi

- Meditation

- Breathing exercises, yogic breathing

- Aromatherapy

- Art classes and pottery

- Nordic walking

- Plant observation

By trying different activities, you will
learn what suits you and how to make
best use of the relaxing influence of the
forest. Take your time to think about
what you like doing. Taking the time
to learn about yourself and about what
you like to do to relax in the forest will
lead you closer to its healing power. Go
too fast and you might miss the way!

Where to do shinrin-yoku

You can forest-bathe anywhere in the
world – wherever there are trees; in hot
weather or in cold; in rain, sunshine or
snow. Japan spreads across a variety of
climate zones, so we have many different
types of forest, from the arctic and subarctic
in the north to the subtropical in the south,
which means that forest-bathers here enjoy
different experiences at different ends of the
country. In the northern regions of Hokkaido
and Tohoku, and parts of Kanto and Chubu,
the main trees are evergreen conifers such
as Sakhalin firs, *yezo* spruces and Sakhalin
spruces. In the cool temperate zone of
Hokkaido and down to Kyushu, the landscape
is full of deciduous beech trees, oak trees
and Pterocarya, a type of walnut tree. These
trees turn beautiful shades of red, orange and
yellow in the autumn, before they shed their
leaves. Evergreen trees like chinquapin and
live oak are a feature of the warm temperate
zone. Camellias and Japanese cinnamon grow
in the coastal areas. In Japan's subtropical
zone in the south, you will find mangroves,
Chinese banyans, strangler figs and evergreen
broad-leaved trees.

You may have a favourite type of
landscape where you will want to
go to practise shinrin-yoku. My
favourite forest base is in Akasawa,
the birthplace of forest-bathing. My
second favourite is Iiyama, where
I conducted the first ever forest-
bathing study, and my third is in
Shinano town.

Iiyama is one of my favourite
forest bases

But, I have visited beautiful forests in
Finland, Australia, Korea and China.
One of my favourite forests in China
is Tianmenshan National Forest Park,
where *Avatar* was filmed. I also love
the Shimen National Forest Park in
Guangzhou city, Guangdong, in South
China. Surrounded by clear water,
and with trees covering 98.9 per cent
of the park, Shimen Park is a green
island paradise. It is some of the only
remaining primary forest in southern
China, and has many rare and precious
plants, such as wild magnolia grandiflora
and wild camellias.

I enjoyed those two forest parks with
all five of my senses: the fragrance of
the forest, the different greens of all the
plants, the murmur of the streams and
the singing of the birds, the taste of the
forest foods and the feel of the trees.

In Finland, I visited the world's first
'well-being'-themed forest, near
Ikaalinen Spa. In this forest, signposts
along the trail focus walkers' attention
on their natural surroundings in order
to induce relaxation and improve mood.

But you don't need such signposts on your forest bath. You don't even need a forest. Once you have learned how to do it, you can do shinrin-yoku anywhere – in a nearby park or in your garden. Look for a place where there are trees, and off you go!

In Japan, some of the things we look for in a forest before we certify it as a healing forest are:

- Temperature of the air

- Humidity

- Luminosity

- Radiant heat

- Air current (wind velocity)

- Sounds (the sound of a waterfall, the whispering of the wind in the trees)

- Volatile organic compounds given off by trees, such as alpha-pinene and D-limonene

- Psychological factors. Is it hot or cold? Light or dark? Is the atmosphere tense or relaxed? Beautiful or ugly? Good or bad? Relaxing or stimulating? Quiet or noisy? Plain or colourful?

And we make sure the forest can
gratify all of your senses.

A certified forest-therapy base in
Japan needs to have more than two
trails, or 'forest-therapy roads'.

You can walk along three different
therapy roads in Chizu, in the Ashizu
valley in western Japan. Chizu is a forest
of cedar and hardwoods, with many
sparkling streams. The scenery changes
with the seasons, from the fresh green
of spring to the rich reds of autumn.
Each trail follows a different section of
the valley and has its own particular
scenery. The Chugoku Nature Trail
follows the route of the old tramcars
that were used for the forestry industry.
The Dam course goes around the Mitaki
Dam, where you can see the mountains
reflected in the water. The third course
winds along the river and has lots of ups
and downs. With its many waterfalls,
the air here is bracing and fresh, full of
negative ions (see page 199).

You can make your own assessment of a forest-therapy path suitable for you by using the criteria below.

- Gentle slopes

- Wide paths

- Well-maintained, well-marked trails

- Free from pollutants

- Far from the noise of traffic

- A stream or waterfall, pond or lake

- Wide variety of plants

- Good luminescence, not too dark

- At least 5km in length

- Plenty of trees, especially evergreens

- Guides or therapists, or forest managers

- Restroom facilities

What if you don't live near a forest? Trees in the city

The importance of trees in the city for public health has been recognized at least since Cyrus the Great planted his famous royal garden in the crowded capital of the Persian empire two and a half thousand years ago. His garden had groves and meadows, fruit trees and cypress trees, roses, lilies and jasmine, all watered by cooling streams and pools, even though it was in the middle of a city. The remains of limestone channels through which the water flowed can still be seen, and stretch almost a kilometre.

Many of our great cities have
wonderful parks and gardens, and
some even have wild areas and woods.
Paris has the Bois de Boulogne;
London has Hyde Park; New York City
has Central Park, which was designed
by the great landscape designer
Frederick Law Olmsted, who said
that 'enjoyment of scenery employs
the mind without fatigue and yet
exercises it; tranquillizes it and yet
enlivens it; and thus, through the
influence of the mind over the body,
gives the effect of refreshing rest and
reinvigoration to the whole system'. In
other words, parks are very relaxing
and restorative places to be.

In Tokyo, we have many beautiful parks. My favourite is Shinjuku Gyoen National Garden, which has many different kinds of trees and flowers. In the north of the park, there is a French garden and an English garden; in the south, the landscape is traditionally Japanese. The park was originally the home of the Naitō family of feudal lords.

The Bois de Boulogne is the second-largest park in Paris

My second favourite is Rikugien Gardens in central Tokyo. *Rikugien* means 'Garden of the Six Principles of Poetry' and the park reproduces in miniature eighty-eight scenes from famous poems. The weeping cherry trees blossom in the spring and in the autumn the park is lit up with the brilliant reds of the maple leaves. It has a large lake in the middle, surrounded by hills and woods. Trails and paths wind through the gardens, lawns and forested areas. These are two of the parks I take my third-year medical students to every Monday for shinrin-yoku.

LEFT: There is a beautiful lake in the Shinjuku Gyoen National Garden in the heart of Tokyo

BELOW: *Rikugien* means 'Garden of the Six Principles of Poetry'

Trees in the city are just as important for our health as trees in the countryside – maybe even more important.

Trees, of course, play a vital part in keeping our cities clean. They help cool the air, reducing the urban 'heat island' effect, and are excellent filters for pollutant gases like carbon monoxide, nitrogen oxides, ozone and sulphur oxides. Another thing that trees are very good at is removing particulate matter from the air, especially if there is frequent rain. The particulates settle on the leaves of trees, much like dust settles on the top of your television. Rain then washes the matter away.

Trees in the city are just as important for our health as trees in the countryside – maybe even more important.

Particulate matter is made up of the
microscopic particles of dust, pollen,
soot and smoke we breathe into our
lungs. Cars are heavy producers of
particulate matter, and people in cities
are exposed to a lot more of it than
those in the countryside. The World
Health Organization (WHO) states that,
of all the air pollutants, fine particulate
matter has the greatest negative effect
on our health, contributing to a higher
incidence of asthma, lung disease,
heart attacks, cancer and strokes. About
90 per cent of people living in cities
are exposed to particulate matter in
concentrations that are higher than those
allowed in the air-quality guidelines set
by the WHO. It was estimated that air
pollution caused 3 million premature
deaths in 2012 and that pollution from
particulate matter will claim 6.2 million
lives a year by 2050, when so many
more of us will be living in cities and
megacities.

A single tree, however, can absorb 4.5kg of air pollutants a year. In 2014, the 'largest tree survey of its kind' calculated that London's trees remove 2,241 tonnes of pollution, store 2,367,000 tonnes of carbon, provide 77,200 tonnes of carbon sequestration, and capture 3,414,000 cubic metres of storm water run-off annually.

Some trees do this more effectively than others. The silver birch, for example, can absorb as much as 50 per cent of the particulate matter produced by cars, which is a lot more than the oak can manage! Scientists in the UK carried out an experiment in a street in Lancaster. First, they measured how much particulate matter got into people's houses (by measuring how much dust settled on their television set). They then planted a row of young silver birch trees along the street. After two weeks, the scientists examined the leaves of the trees with a special electron microscope; the leaves are covered with tiny hairs, and it is these hairs that trap the particulate matter from passing cars. At the end of the experiment, the televisions were 50 per cent less dusty than they were at the beginning.

Silver birch trees are particularly good at absorbing the pollution from cars

How to do shinrin-yoku in the park

1. Leave behind your phone, camera, music and any other distractions

2. Leave behind your expectations

3. Slow down; forget about the time

4. Come into the present moment

5. Find a spot to sit – on the grass, beside a tree or on a park bench

6. Notice what you can hear and see

7. Notice what you feel

8. Stay for two hours if possible (though you will begin to notice the effects after twenty minutes)

Sound

Sssh. Listen. What do you hear? Yes,
that's right – aeroplanes overhead, cars,
motorcycles, construction work, the
refrigerator, the air conditioning, someone's
phone ringing with that annoying ringtone.
Your own phone ringing!

It is difficult to find peace and quiet in
today's world. Can you remember the last
time you heard – nothing?

Noise isn't just annoying. It can increase
blood pressure, interfere with concentration
and sleep and lead to forgetfulness. It has
been found to retard the development
of reading and verbal skills in children.
Chronic noise is stressful. And we know
what stress causes . . . a whole host of
health problems.

More than half the world's population now
lives in a noisy city. Around 80 million
Europeans live with noise levels that are
judged too high. More than 11 million
Americans are exposed to traffic noise so
high they risk hearing loss.

And although Japan may seem to
be the land of serenity, peace and
quiet, it is in fact a nation of noise.
According to a study by the WHO,
Japan is the noisiest nation in the
world. From 7 a.m. to 10 p.m.,
seven days a week, Japan is assailed
by announcements, warnings and
reminders, bells, chimes, sirens and
tunes. There are loudspeakers in
train stations and carriages, talking
escalators and cash-points. Street
vendors shout through megaphones
and shops employ staff to welcome
you in the loudest voice they can
manage. *Irrashaimase! Welcome!* Local
governments make non-stop
announcements telling schoolchildren
it's time to go home, or to remind us
that it's a public holiday tomorrow.
Loudspeakers on the tops of rubbish
trucks announce, 'The garbage truck is
coming. The garbage truck is coming,'
then play a few bars of a tune called
'Coming through the Rye'.

Japan has regulations on acceptable noise levels, but they are not very well enforced. The level of outdoor noise is often in excess of the 70-decibel limit.

Perhaps we are addicted to noise. Restaurants pipe out music, the radio blares in coffee shops. Think how many of us keep the television on all day or listen to music constantly through earphones. And we all know people who feel they have to talk all the time, so afraid of silence that they have to fill it.

Natural silence

With such high levels of noise everywhere, most people no longer have the opportunity to enjoy the restorative sounds of peace and quiet. Natural silence has been called one of the most endangered resources on the planet.

Silence is considered such a precious commodity that the US National Park Service has put a protection order on it. In the middle of the Hoh Rainforest in Olympic National Park in Washington state is a small red stone that marks 'one square inch of silence', the focal point of a campaign to create a place that is totally free of man-made noise.

Natural silence has been called one of the most endangered resources on the planet.

It is hard to imagine a more peaceful place. The park has some of the largest temperate rainforest in the western hemisphere. It is a long wild coastline with snow-capped mountains and deep valleys. It is the quietest place in America and one of the most untouched and ecologically diverse. The hope of the campaign is that by listening to one square inch of silence we will learn to become true listeners to our environment and to value natural silence once again.

The Hoh Rainforest in the US has a small red stone that marks 'one square inch of silence'

Of course, silence in nature does not always mean total quiet. When you are free from human noise you have an opportunity to listen to the sounds that only nature provides.

In order to help combat noise pollution, the Ministry of the Environment in Japan has recorded and archived a hundred Japanese sounds. Among the sounds is the lovely creaking, rustling and knocking noise of the Sagano bamboo forest as the wind passes through it. This forest is one of the most peaceful and meditative soundscapes to be found anywhere in the world – and yet it is only half an hour from the busy, noisy centre of Kyoto city.

The soundscape project has also preserved the roaring of the water at Shōmyō Falls, the tallest waterfall in Japan; the rushing sound of the Chigamigawa river in Kagoshima; the songs of little birds in Enrei, Okaya; and the calls of wild birds on the lake at the foot of Mount Fuji.

The Sagano bamboo forest is only half an hour from Kyoto city

It has captured the sounds of the Noshiro pinewoods rustling, the wind in the reed fields at the mouth of the Kitakami river, and the buzzing of the cicadas in the mountain temple of Yamadera, which inspired Matsuo Bashō in the seventeenth century to write his famous haiku:

Silence
The song of the cicadas
Penetrates the rocks.

If there was one natural sound you could preserve for ever, what would it be?

The Shōmyō Falls is the tallest waterfall in Japan

In Japanese, there are many onomatopoeic words for the sounds of nature:

shito shito: the sound of light rain

zā zā: the sound of heavy rain

kasa kasa: the light sound of leaves rustling underfoot

gasa gasa: the heavy rustling of branches swaying in the wind

hyū hyū: the sound of the wind blowing

goro goro: the rumble of thunder

saku saku: the crunching sound of snow underfoot

Tuning into nature to relax

Often, when I do shinrin-yoku, I am accompanied by the constant sound of running water. There is the buzzing of the cicadas all summer long and the *kenkenkenkenken* of the pheasant in the spring. The wind blows and rustles the leaves. There may be the crash of a waterfall in the distance, or the song of a bush warbler just above my head. The silence of the natural world is in fact a constant, wondrous, never-ending symphony.

> The silence of the natural world is in fact a constant, wondrous, never-ending symphony.

The sounds of nature are a link to the environment and to ourselves. In the forest, we can learn once again to listen to the landscape we were built to hear. When we are quiet we can tune in to the natural world. Immersed in nature, we are in a whole new dimension, a restorative sonic landscape. Being still and quiet, we can hear the sound of silence and begin to relax.

Studies have repeatedly shown that we prefer the sounds of nature to the sounds of urban noise, that the sounds of nature relieve stress and that we feel relaxed when we can hear birdsong or running water. Researchers at Brighton and Sussex Medical School (UK) investigating the connection between the brain, the body and background noise, looked at what happened in people's brains while they listened to a series of sounds from either natural or man-made environments.

While they listened, the participants
had to perform a cognitive task. Their
heart rates were monitored as well as
their nervous systems, blood pressure,
metabolism and digestion as they
listened. The results showed that when
the participants listened to artificial
sounds, their attention was focused
inwards. Inward-focused attention is
associated with worry and brooding.
When they listened to the sounds of
nature, they turned their attention
outwards. In addition, participants did
less well on their tests when they were
listening to man-made noise. The nature
sounds decreased the functioning of
the body's sympathetic nervous system
('fight or flight') and increased the
parasympathetic system ('rest and
recover'), indicating that we are more
relaxed when we listen to nature.

We are
more
relaxed
when we
listen to
nature.

Another study, this time using a virtual-reality forest, found that including the sound of the forest with the projection was more restorative and stress-relieving than when the forest was shown without sound.

The sounds of nature we like most are:

- Water

- Wind

- Bird chatter

- Birdsong

People are most sensitive to sounds between the frequencies of 2,500 and 3,500 hertz. This is also the range that birds sing in, which might explain why birdsong sounds like music to us!

Cognitive quiet

The sounds of the forest soothe our
frazzled heads, lift us out of mental
fatigue and give us the silence
in which to think. When we do
shinrin-yoku, we can find the peace
and serenity that Japan was once
famous for. In the forest, we can let
our ears be captured by the sounds
of the natural world and have our
senses refreshed and rejuvenated.

How to be still and listen to the sounds of nature

Tuning in to the sounds of nature can be hard. We are so used to noise. Even when we are quiet, there is the noise of our thoughts inside our heads. In fact, it is when we are still and quiet that the internal noise starts up. Our thoughts go round and round and it is not easy to quieten them.

1. **Start by slowing down.** You need to give yourself some time: it takes time to let go of your thoughts and hear natural silence. Find a spot and sit down.

2. **Focus on your breath**. If unwanted thoughts creep in, concentrate on breathing deeply. When you breathe out, let any distractions float away.

3. **Listen in all directions**. After a while, the noise inside your head will quieten down and you will begin to hear the sounds of nature. Notice what you can hear. The tap tap tap of a beak on wood? The two-tone notes of a birdcall? See if you can listen further.

4. **Close your eyes to help you hear more intensely**. Remaining still and quiet and paying attention to the sounds of nature will open your ears. All you have to do is be quiet and listen. If you listen hard enough, maybe you can hear the voices of the trees talking to each other in their phytoncide language. Start by slowing down . . .

Sight

Our sense of sight has been called
the most important of all our senses.
We are visual creatures and perceive
most of our impressions through our
eyes. It is with our sense of sight that
we experience the splendour and
beauty of the natural world.

There is a Japanese word, *komorebi*,
which has no direct equivalent in
English. It roughly translates as 'the
sunlight filtering through the leaves
in the trees'. It is made up of three
kanji, or characters.

The first kanji (木) means 'tree' or
'trees'; the second one (漏) means
'escape' or 'leaking through'; the
third (日) is 'light' or 'sun'.

The word is also used for the
interplay of leaves and light in the
shadows on the ground beneath
the trees. The closest equivalent in
English is probably 'dappled sunlight'.

It is with
our sense of
sight that we
experience
the splendour
and beauty
of the natural
world.

Komorebi is particularly beautiful when
the sun is low, or if there is an early
mist or a light fog. I never fail to feel
restored and rejuvenated by this magical
sight. And don't we all feel cheered
on a beautiful sunny day when the
sun makes patterns on the pavement
beneath a city tree?

Sadly, there is generally not much
komorebi in our everyday lives. The most
light many of us see each day is the
glow of a screen. We look at our phones
when we wake up in the morning and
usually last thing at night before we go
to sleep. In the hours in between, we
are in front of our computers, working,
sending emails, watching films and
updating our Facebook pages. In our
offices, we are often required to sit at
a screen all day long.

Our eyes are less good at filtering out the artificial light we spend our days looking at than they are at filtering out the ultraviolet light of sunshine. Digital screens, LED and fluorescent lighting all emit blue light, which contains more energy than red or orange light and is known as high-energy light. But while blue light helps to keep us awake during daylight hours, constant exposure in our offices and from our devices can add up. The more time we spend in artificial light, the more discomfort we can experience. Our eyes weren't designed to look at screens, and long hours at our computers can cause headaches, eye strain and technostress.

Our eyes weren't designed to look at cityscapes either. Studies on the effect of colours on emotions have shown that we find the blues and greens of nature the most restful. They make us less anxious and reduce our stress. The greys of an urban scene, however, have been shown to make us unhappier and more aggressive.

Of course, for most of our existence, humans have been surrounded by green. Nature is what we have been accustomed to looking at. We are reassured by green on a very primitive level. Where there is green, there is water. And where there is water, we can find food. When the world around us contains plenty of green, we can relax, knowing we are not going to go hungry. No wonder the colour green can have such a positive impact.

But nature is not just green, it's also beautiful. Nature creates beautiful patterns everywhere we look: in the petals of a flower, in the branches of a snowflake, in the spirals of a shell. There are patterns in everything, from the bracts of a pine cone to the arrangement of leaves and the way a fern unfolds.

These natural patterns are called fractals. They are seen in ocean waves, lightning, coastlines and rivers, as well as in flowers, trees, clouds and snowflakes. A fractal is a pattern that repeats itself over and over again and looks the same at any scale. They are everywhere in nature. Think of the way a tree grows. One trunk grows until it divides into two branches, then the two branches divide into another two, and those two divide into another two, and so on. The pattern of a little twig is, in the end, the same as the pattern of a giant hinoki. No matter what scale you look at it on, the patterns of the branches will be the same.

A snowflake is an example of a fractal pattern

These infinite patterns of nature are scientifically proven to relax us, no matter how complicated the pattern may become. Richard Taylor, Professor of Physics, Psychology and Art at the Materials Science Institute in Oregon, has done a huge amount of research on what happens when we look at fractal patterns, using eye-tracking equipment and machines that measure brain activity. He has found that we are 'hard wired' to respond to the kind of fractals found in nature – and that looking at these kinds of natural patterns can reduce our stress by as much as 60 per cent.

Looking at natural fractal patterns can reduce our stress by as much as 60 per cent.

What Professor Taylor has discovered is that we are visually fluent in the patterns of the natural world. Because we evolved in the scenery of the natural world, we can process its patterns easily. And it is this fluency that relaxes us. We enjoy looking at the patterns in nature because we are good at it!

However, patterns in nature do more than simply relax and comfort us. They can also amaze us and fill us with awe. As Aristotle said, 'In all things of nature there is something of the marvellous.' Many people think that it is precisely this sense of being awestruck that makes us feel better in the forest.

The Nobel Prize-winning psychologist Dr Dacher Keltner describes awe as 'the feeling of being in the presence of something vast or beyond human scale that transcends our current understanding of things'. It is when we are filled with awe at the sight of nature that we begin to think about things outside ourselves. A sense of awe helps us to slow down and stop worrying. It transforms negative emotions into positive feelings. It gives us pause and brings us joy.

A sense of awe gives us pause and brings us joy.

Exercise:

Use fractals to make you feel happier

Go to the forest, a park or just into your garden, and find a spot to sit.

Look up at the clouds and the sky, or at the ripples on the surface of a pond. Look at the water trickling in a stream or the way the branches in a tree divide.

Go in close and look at the veins in a leaf or the petals in a flower and notice the patterns.

Soon you will start to see patterns all around you.

Notice your stress levels before and afterwards and see how the fractal patterns in nature can make you feel more relaxed.

When you see how much of the world around you is patterned, you will begin to feel the awe and splendour of the natural world. And that will bring you joy as well as a sense of calm!

Smell

Of all our senses, our sense of smell
is the most primal. None of our other
senses has such a direct effect on our
minds and bodies. Smells affect our
mood and our behaviour; they are
connected to our emotions and to
our memories. A smell can trigger
an immediate response and have an
effect that lasts long after it has gone.

One of the most powerful elements
of shinrin-yoku is the fragrance
the trees release, their phytoncides.
When you walk in the forest, you are
breathing in its healing power. All
you have to do is be there.

When you
walk in
the forest,
you are
breathing in
its healing
power.

What the forest smells like

The fragrance of your forest will depend on what trees grow there. Different trees have different smells – of course. There is great variety in the aromas of trees. Some have a cool, pungent smell; some a deep, woody scent. Many spruces and firs have a lemony aroma or can smell of turpentine. Some can smell sharp and refreshing; some may even have a slightly salty fragrance.

Some of our most aromatic trees are conifers. They have needles for leaves and are mostly evergreen, so they stay green all year round, unlike trees with flat leaves, which fall in the autumn with new ones returning in the spring. Conifers can live for hundreds of years – some for thousands! Coniferous trees were the first aromatic plants on earth, appearing 300 million years ago. So, when we walk in a coniferous forest, we have a chance to smell what the world smelled like right back at the beginning of time.

Hinoki

The smell of Japanese cypress, or *hinoki*, is my favourite tree smell. It is a beautiful fresh, lemony, slightly smoky aroma. For many Japanese, it is the smell of home. You can't avoid the smell of *hinoki* if you live in Japan. You will smell it everywhere, not just in the forest. We use it to build our houses, temples and shrines and also the wooden *rotenburo* baths in our hot springs. So we, quite literally, bathe in it.

The smell of the *hinoki* tree is everywhere in Japan

Scots pine

One of the most widely distributed conifers in the world is the Scots pine, so you might well know its herby, fresh, piney smell. The scent of a Scots pine is a strong and dry fragrance, sometimes a bit like turpentine. Aromatherapists use the essential oil of the Scots pine to ease mental and physical fatigue, to clear a cluttered mind and to sharpen focus.

The Scots pine is one of the most widely distributed conifers in the world

Spruce trees have a darker and earthier fragrance than pine trees

Spruce

The smell of spruce is similar to that of pine, but it is darker and earthier. Aromatherapists say it has a grounding effect and can encourage a sense of expansiveness.

Douglas fir

The Douglas fir has an intense citrus fragrance. It is a rich and resinous smell. The essential oil of a Douglas fir is used by aromatherapists to aid relaxation. Its effects on the mind and body are said to be similar to those brought about by meditation.

The essential oil of a Douglas fir is said to help relax you

Cedar tree

If you peel a piece of bark from a
cedar tree, you will release a deep
and mysterious smell. The scent of
a cedar tree is often described as
woody and earthy or spicy, and like
balsam. It is a warm, resinous smell
and can be very sweet.

The essential oils of cedar trees
come from the wood rather than
from the needles and twigs, like
other evergreen trees. The smell
of the wood is said to repel moths
and insects such as fleas, ants and
mosquitoes – which is why linen
chests are often made from cedarwood. Early Egyptians used it for
perfume, as well as for embalming.
The high oil content of the wood
stops it from decaying. Some of the
oldest wooden structures in the
world are made from cedarwood.
Sweet-wood oils have been used in
meditation and devotional practices
since ancient times; the cedar tree
was used to build King Solomon's
temple because its beautiful fragrance
was thought to encourage prayer and
lead worshippers closer to God.

The modern source of most cedarwood oil is in fact a juniper tree known as red cedar, which has a sharper smell, the smell of freshly sharpened pencils. Unsurprisingly, since red cedar is used to make pencils!

The essential oils of cedar trees come from the wood and not from the needles and twigs

The fragrance of cedarwood is said to relax the nerves and calm the spirit. Aromatherapists use it to stimulate emotional strength and to promote feelings of self-acceptance.

Ponderosa pine

A pine tree with a different kind of smell is the ponderosa pine, which grows on the dry, rocky slopes in the Black Hills and across the Rocky Mountains in the US and smells like baking biscuits. It has a black bark that peels off when the tree is about 120 years old (a mere teenager, in ponderosa terms) to reveal a yellow under-layer which the locals call 'yellow belly'. This yellow underbelly of the ponderosa smells of cinnamon, butterscotch and vanilla. Yum.

The yellow inside of ponderosa pines smells of cinnamon, butterscotch and vanilla

Each tree and each forest has a unique fragrance. Do some research on the trees in your local forest and experience their smell for yourself the next time you forest-bathe. How would you describe the smell?

If the leaves on the trees in your forest fall in winter, then your forest is deciduous. There are no essential oils from deciduous woodland trees, but the scent of leaves, soil and moss is therapeutic all the same.

Four Japanese tree essential oils

Hinoki (Chamaecyparis obtusa), Japanese cypress

In Japanese, hinoki means cypress. Hi means 'fire' and ki means 'tree' so hinoki is also known as 'fire tree', because it is used to make the fire in Shinto shrines. It is one of the Five Sacred Trees of Kiso and the wood is used to build the Ise Shrine, Japan's most sacred Shinto shrine.

The essential oil is distilled from the dark red-brown wood and has a woody aroma. The aromatic effect on the mind is said to be relaxing, calming and grounding. Aromatherapists also use it to relieve aching muscles. You could try adding two to three drops of hinoki oil to your bathwater to soothe aches and pains. Or you can do as I do, and diffuse it all through the winter to keep away colds and flu.

Put two drops of oil into your hands and breathe in the smell to lift your mood and give you energy.

The essential oil is distilled from the aromatic bark of the tree and can be used to relieve aches and pains

Hiba (*Thujopsis dolabrata*)

The Japanese consider the *hiba* to be a sacred tree. It is also highly valued for its smell, which is said to be repel insects. There is a Japanese saying, 'In houses made from *hiba* wood, mosquitoes will stay away for three years.'

The essential oil is distilled from the wood rather than from the leaves and has a smoky, woody scent that is a bit like cedarwood. In aromatherapy, it is used to ease anxiety and relax the body, and can be diffused throughout the night to aid sleep.

The Japanese consider the *Hiba* to be a sacred tree

Hokkaido momi (*Abies sachalinensis*)

The Hokkaido momi is an evergreen fir tree that grows in northern Hokkaido and on Sakhalin island. The oil is distilled from the leaves and branches, and firs from Sakhalin produce more essential oil than any other Japanese conifer.

The Hokkaido momi is regarded as a symbol of the power of life because you can see the leaves of the tree even when they are covered by snow. In aromatherapy, Hokkaido momi oil is used to calm the nerves and relieve stress. It is also used for respiratory conditions.

Even when covered in snow, you can still see the green leaves of the *momi* trees in Hokkaido

Sugi (Cryptomeria japonica)

The *sugi* is the national tree of Japan, with a light, sweet fragrance.

You can make the essential oil from both the leaves and the wood. Aromatherapists use it for emotional support, and to ease respiratory conditions and muscular aches and pains. The *sugi* tree can grow for hundreds of years, and some are thousands of years old. Because of this, some people say that the oil from the tree is a reminder that our souls live for ever.

The Japanese *sugi* pine is sometimes called the Japanese red cedar because of its red-brown bark

Another favourite smell in Japan

Another smell that the Japanese
love is the smell of the tiny orange-
yellow flowers of the kinmokusei tree.
This tree is everywhere in Japan
and comes into bloom at the end of
summer. The kinmokusei is also known
as the kuriko tree, or '9-ri fragrance'.
Nine ri is about 4.5km – the
distance this lovely smell can travel!

For more on the properties of
essential oils, turn to page 231.

The distinctive flowers of
the kinmokusei tree have a
wonderful smell

The smell of the earth

There are other smells in the air in the forest, for example the smell of the soil, and the smell of rain.

Do you remember the soil microbe that I talked about in the previous chapter, the harmless common bacteria M. *vaccae*? Well, this has a smell, too. Scientists call this smell geosmin, and it is the dirt smell that gives beetroot and carrots that earthy taste.

In fact, many types of food can have this earthy taste and smell. The French call it *terroir*, or the taste of the region – or, more precisely, the taste of the region's microbes. You can taste it in wine and cheese. You can even taste it in chocolate.

The smell is stronger if the weather has been dry for a long time. Humans are very sensitive to geosmin; it is said we are able to detect it at levels as low as five parts per trillion. It is thought that, during our evolution, it was this chemical that helped us to find food, especially after a period of drought.

Then there is that delicious fresh smell of the forest after it has rained. When it is dry for a long time, plant oils collect in the soil and rocks. This is one of the plants' ways of surviving during a long spell of dry weather. When it rains, the water releases the oils that have been stored in the rock and the fragrance fills the air.

There is a name for this smell, too. Scientists call it petrichor, from the Greek words *petra*, meaning 'stone', and *ichor*, which refers to the essence that flows instead of blood in the veins of the gods. So petrichor literally means 'the essence of rock'. The smell of life!

Negative ions

The smells of the forest are an essential part of why we feel so good there. But there is something else in the air that is said to make us feel better when we are in nature and which we can't actually smell – and that is negative air ions.

Ions are charged particles in the air. They can be positively charged or negatively charged. Negative ions are the good ones and are said to have energizing and refreshing effects, and to help increase mental clarity and our sense of well-being. There are many more negative ions outdoors than there are indoors. And they are particularly abundant in forests and near waterfalls, rivers and streams.

The air near a waterfall can contain as many as 100,000 negative ions per cubic centimetre, whereas the air in your office might have only a few 100 per cubic centimetre. So it's no wonder a walk by a waterfall can feel so invigorating! If you can walk where there is a stream or a river, you will maximize your intake of negative ions and boost your energy levels.

Negative ions help increase mental clarity and our sense of well-being.

Breathing in the forest

The breath is one of the easiest paths to our central nervous system, and some forest-bathing centres in Japan hold classes where you can practise yogic breathing.

Yogic breathing helps to create a sense of calm. It decreases our heart rate and blood pressure and relaxes our muscles and is a good way to increase your intake of the forest's natural aromatherapy.

Exercise:

Mountain pose and breath in the forest

Stand with your arms facing outwards. Breathe in through your nose and, as you inhale, slowly raise your arms until your hands meet above your head. Hold the pose for a count of four. Then reach higher and, raising yourself on to your toes, rotate your hands to face outwards. Begin, slowly, to breathe out while you lower your arms. When you are back at your starting position, fill your lungs deeply once again with the fresh air of the forest. Do this three times.

Touch

It is with our sense of touch that we can begin to physically and literally reconnect with nature.

Hippocrates wrote: 'Illnesses do not come upon us out of the blue. They are developed from the small daily sins against nature. When enough sins have accumulated, illnesses will suddenly appear.' Many of our illnesses, stresses and anxieties are due to a lack of connection with nature. Taking a hands-on approach to the natural world will help to restore that connection. Feel the breeze on your face, let the water of a stream ripple through your hands, lie on the ground, take your shoes off and go barefoot.

Onsen

In Japan, we can immerse ourselves literally in the healing power of nature in our famous hot springs, or onsen.

Japan has been called the world's hot-spring superpower. There are 27,000 in Japan, pumping out water from underground volcanic sources into a bathing pool. Nearly half of this water is over 42 degrees Celsius.

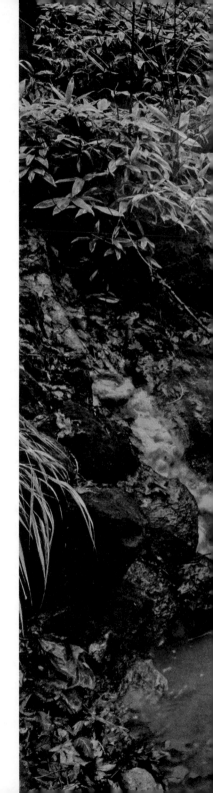

Around 1,300 years ago, the author of
the *Izumi no Kuni Fudoki* (*The Chronicle of the
Land of Izumo*) wrote about the hot spring
in Tamatsukuri in Shimane prefecture:
'Bathing just once in this hot spring will
clear your skin, and continued bathing
will cure all your aches and pains. Given
such positive results without exception
since long ago, people call it the "water
of the gods".'

Beauty and health without medicine or
cosmetics – no wonder *onsen* bathing is
so popular. In Europe as well as Japan,
hot springs are known as 'the fountains
of youth' because of their abilities to
rejuvenate and restore.

The Kinosaki onsen is one of Japan's
most popular hot springs

The water that spouts up from underground is called *gensen kakenagashi*, or 'water flowing from the source'. The water that flows from the source is said to be the most healing.

The original hot-spring doctor was Gotō Konzan. About three hundred years ago, Konzan developed a theory that the root cause of all sickness was a blockage in the flow of energy in the body. He recommended releasing that blocked flow by soaking in a hot spring, and the hotter the better. The hot spring he chose for his treatment was hidden away in a secluded valley, but its fame spread and the Kinosaki *onsen*, in Hyōgo prefecture, is still one of Japan's favourite hot-spring areas – even though it is difficult to get to!

Grounding yourself in nature

If you can't end your forest bath with a
hot-spring bath, there is something else
you can do to connect with the earth
and keep the flow of energy between
your body and the natural world. Take
your shoes off!

Have you ever noticed how good it feels
to walk barefoot on sand or grass or soil?
This is not just because of the relief you
feel when you take off your stiff shoes
or your high heels. It is because, when
your bare feet touch the ground, you are
receiving a dose of the earth's powerful
healing electrons.

Let's think of the earth like a giant
battery. It has a natural low-level
electrical charge. Whenever we do
anything with electrics, like wiring up a
plug or fixing a light fitting, we always
have to make sure that it is safe by
connecting it to the earth. We talk about
electrics being 'earthed' or 'grounded'.

And human beings are the same. We
know exactly what we mean when we
describe someone as grounded: solid,
strong, balanced and centred. This is
what our bodies are like, too, when
we bring them into contact with the
electrical charge of the earth. As we
evolved, we were in constant contact
with the electrical energy of the earth.
When we are electrically grounded, we
are in harmony with nature.

Alas, our modern lives have
disconnected us from our natural
electrical source. Many of us live and
work in buildings that seem to aim for
the sky. Our tall offices and apartment
blocks may give us spectacular views,
but they have removed us even further
from the surface of the earth. Not many
of us choose to sleep on the ground
these days and, when we go outside,
we protect our feet from the earth
with shoes!

Our ancestors wore shoes that were made of animal skins or wood. Shoes made of leather conduct electrons and so maintain the electrical connection between us and the earth. Rubber-soled shoes, however, do not. When we wear shoes that insulate us from the ground, we are blocking the flow of electrons and breaking the connection with the earth that helps our bodies to function properly.

Some people have called shoes one of the most dangerous inventions of mankind and maintain that walking barefoot is the way we are meant to get around.

Going barefoot

Luckily, there is a very easy way to become grounded. All we have to do is walk barefoot for a while, preferably on sand, earth or grass. Grounding exercises are easy:

1. First, take off your socks and shoes and go outside

2. Stand on the earth, grass or sand

3. You need two points of contact to form an electrical circuit, so it's best to stand with both feet on the ground. If you are lying down, you can make a circuit with one foot and one elbow

4. For best results, stay grounded for twenty minutes every day

5. Be careful to avoid glass and try not to stand on grass that has been sprayed with pesticides

Want to go further? Here are two grounding techniques that earthing specialists recommend:

1. While barefoot outside, sit or stand and focus all your attention on the soles of your feet, paying attention to what you can feel

2. Stand with your feet parallel and shoulder-width apart. Keep your chin tucked in and your spine straight. Let your arms hang loose. Standing straight, let all your tension and weight sink into your feet. Imagine roots spreading out from the bottom of your feet into the earth beneath you

Many people like to forest-bathe barefoot. Walking in the forest without shoes will help to restore the broken connection between you and the natural world. But if you don't want to take your shoes off, make sure you make contact with nature some other way. Plunge your hands into a pile of leaves, pick up a pebble from the bottom of a stream, enjoy the sensation of the breeze against your skin, or lean against a tree and – yes! – you can put your arms around it.

Taste

Another way of connecting with the forest is to eat or drink it.

Many restaurants and shops in forest-therapy bases and trails in Japan provide forest-therapy meals. Forest-therapy meals are prepared using ingredients that are grown locally so that you can taste the region you are walking in. They are also carefully considered from a nutritional point of view. Your bento-box lunch might include plants that help boost the immune system, for example, or ones that provide plenty of vitamin D. This is not fast food; it is very slow food.

Wild mountain food, or *sansai*

Forests are full of food – you just have
to know where to look and what to
look for.

The Japanese word *sansai* means
'mountain vegetables'. *Sansai* grow
wild in marshes and grasslands, or
in the forest. The Japanese have been
gathering wild food to cook with since
ancient times. In fact, wild plants, or
sansai, have helped the Japanese on
many occasions when food has been
scarce because of drought or some
other natural disaster. When food was
in short supply after the Second World
War, city dwellers scoured the hills for
tasty *sansai* such as *warabi* (bracken),
tara-no-me (angelica) and *kogomi*
(a type of fern).

These days, many Japanese look forward to the *sansai* season in spring and summer and take to the forests to search out delicious food that nature provides for free. You can do all sorts of things with *sansai*; it's not just for salad. Some wild plants can be boiled or fried, some cooked in soup or as tempura, some turned into pickles and jam.

You might recognize some Japanese *sansai*, like *renkon*, or lotus root, which is found in many traditional Japanese dishes. Bamboo shoots are another familiar wild food. Many people go on *sansai* expeditions in June to pick *takenoko*, or baby bamboo. In winter, people gather the giant bamboo sprouts, *moso*, just as they are poking through the ground.

Some *sansai* gatherers can be very secretive about where their favourite wild foods grow. You might not find anyone who is willing to tell you where to find Japanese angelica buds, a delicacy known as 'king of *sansai*'.

Eight Japanese *sansai*

1. A favourite Japanese wild plant is *yabu-kanzō*, a kind of day lily, which you see in early spring. You can cook it in a soup or make tempura with it. When fried, it tastes of onion

2. *Fuki* (butterbur) is a bitter but very versatile plant. It is a bit like rhubarb and has soft, fat stems. You can cook it with miso and rice

3. *Mitsuba* is a very popular *sansai* in spring. It has a similar flavour to parsley and is typically used in salads and soups

4. *Zenmai* (Japanese royal fern) is high in potassium and vitamins A and C. It is usually fried and served as a side dish with wild sesame

5. *Warabi* is a fern that grows in the forest. You can eat the stems and make a starch from the roots, which the Japanese use for the delicious chewy summer pudding *warabimochi*

6. *Azami* is a popular *sansai* in the summer. It can be eaten with miso soup or pickled as a preserve

7. Maybe it will surprise you to know that you can eat Japanese knotweed! *Itadori* is a very common edible weed in Japan. The new shoots appear in late winter and are used in many dishes

8. *Katakuri* is a lily that is found wild in the mountains. You can eat the bulb and the roots. It is used in many traditional Japanese dishes, from soups to tempura.

The Japanese have known the nutritional value of many of these plants for generations, but *sansai* offer more than just vitamins. When you eat wild mountain food, you are taking in the energy of the earth as well.

WARNING:
Be very careful when foraging for wild food. There are plenty of poisonous plants, and they often resemble edible ones. Never eat anything you have picked in the wild that you are not 100 per cent certain is safe to eat.

Forest-bathing tea ceremony

Shinrin-yoku walks often end with a drink of tea brewed from the twigs, leaves, flowers or bark of the trees and plants in the forest. I think this is a lovely final ritual, a way of incorporating the forest, bringing us into harmony with the natural world, just like in a traditional Japanese tea ceremony.

Chanoyu:

The way of tea

The traditional Japanese tea ceremony is called
Chanoyu, which translates, literally, as 'hot
water for tea'. It is also known as Sadō or
Chado, which translates as 'the way of tea'.
The way of tea is both an artistic ritual of
preparing and serving Japanese green tea and
a spiritual discipline designed to bring about
inner peace through harmony with nature.
The four principles of tea are harmony, respect,
purity and tranquillity.

At the heart of the way of tea is the concept
ichi-go ichi-e, which translates literally as
'one time, one meeting', so 'for this time only'
or 'one chance in a lifetime'. Another way to
translate ichi-go ichi-e is 'live each moment
to the full because today is all we have'.
Everything in the tea ceremony is focused on
the preparation of the tea, the cleaning of the
tools and the aesthetic appreciation of the
ritual. Very little conversation is allowed, other
than discussion about the ceremony itself.

Instead, the participants are mindful that every moment is unique and should be lived to the full. Chanoyu is not a tea party. It is a quiet, meditative tradition of preparing a bowl of tea from the heart.

The sixteenth-century tea master Sen no Rikyū laid down the seven rules of Chanoyu:

1. Make a delicious bowl of tea

2. Lay the charcoal so the water boils efficiently

3. Arrange the flowers as they are in the field

4. Keep the tea room cool in the summer and warm in the winter

5. Do everything ahead of time

6. Be prepared for rain

7. Be considerate of other guests

These are also profound rules for life, reminding us to live fully with our hearts and minds, to enjoy the simplicity of the natural world, and to be prepared, thoughtful and kind.

Evergreen-tree tea

All sorts of leaves, flowers and bark can be used to make tea, and many will have medicinal properties, too. If you know that the plant is completely safe, pick a few leaves or twigs while you are on your walk and brew up a cup of tea at the end of your forest bath.

While I was looking for recipes for this book, I came across some recipes for tea made from the needles of spruces, firs and pines. These evergreen coniferous trees are all good sources of vitamins A and C. Given the strong smell of lemon they can give off, it didn't surprise me to read that pine needles can have as much as five times the amount of vitamin C as a lemon and eight times as much as an orange. This makes them useful teas to drink in the winter season to help fight off colds, but because the trees are evergreens, you will be able to forage them for tea all year round. The flavours of needle teas vary from fruity and resinous to lemony sharp, smoky and herbal. Young needles have a gentler flavour than older ones, which can be bitter.

Water

Let's not forget the delicious fresh taste of mountain water.

There are many springs and streams from which we can drink in Japan and at least two hundred of them are protected by the Ministry of the Environment as Exquisite and Well-conserved Waters. These are called *meisui* in Japanese, which means 'good water'.

Many of these *meisui* are springs and rivers from which Japanese people have been drinking since ancient times. Unsurprisingly, some of the springs that produce the most water are at the foot of Mount Fuji, the highest mountain in Japan. One group of springs produces a million cubic metres of water a day.

When you are on your forest walk, look out for a fresh-water spring or stream from which the water is good to drink. Make a cup of your hands and drink in the forest! And if there is nothing to eat and drink in your forest, just breathe deeply. You will still be able to enjoy the taste of fresh air.

The Sixth Sense

Nature feeds our souls and brings us joy.

Many people think we have more than five senses – some people think we have eight or twelve. But most of us agree on some ineffable extra sense, a sixth sense with which we connect with the world beyond ourselves. Perhaps this is our sense for happiness.

This is what we feel in nature that can be so hard to describe – a feeling of wonder and excitement, transcendence and even ecstasy. And the more trees there are, the more likely we are to feel it. Indeed, studies have shown that the greater the scenic beauty, the more happiness we feel.

It is when we connect to nature with all our senses that the magic happens and our lives can be transformed. Immersed in the natural world, we can experience the miracle of life and connect to something larger than ourselves. Nature takes our breath away and breathes new life into us.

Nature takes our breath away and breathes new life into us.

In fact, the sense of connectedness
with nature not only floods us with
joy in the moment, it can teach us to
be happy in the future! Researchers
in Canada have shown that our sense
of connectedness to nature can
enhance our capacity for happiness.
Connectedness to nature can even
predict how happy we can feel. In
other words, if you have been happy
in the forest today, you will find
happiness tomorrow.

There is something in nature that
can make us happy that is separate
from the happiness we get from other
things, like friends, or family, or music.
Our relationship with nature is unique,
and it can make us uniquely happy.
When you can feel that joy in nature,
then you are truly forest-bathing!

Exercise:

Finding your feelings in the forest

When you are in the forest, notice your emotional response to being there

Start by closing your eyes. See if you can feel which way you want to walk. Use your intuition

Notice all the sensual pleasures of the forest

What do you feel when you hear the breeze in the trees and the songs of the birds?

What do you feel when you look at the trees around you?

What do you feel when you smell the forest fragrance?

What do you feel when the sun warms your face, or you lie on the ground?

What do you feel when you taste the fresh air?

Let time drop away and, with it, all your worldly worries

What do you feel now?

My top tips for forest-bathing

- An optimum time to spend in the forest is around four hours, during which time you should aim to walk about 5km. But shorter bursts work, too. If you only have the morning, why not try a two-hour walk of about 2.5km?

- If you feel tired, you can take a rest anywhere and any time you like

- If you feel thirsty, you can drink water or tea, anywhere and any time you like

- Find a place in the forest you like. Then, you can sit for a while and read, or just enjoy the beautiful scenery

- Choose the forest-bathing path that suits your needs

- If you want to give your immune system a powerful boost, go for a three-day/two-night forest-bathing trip

- Forest-bathing is a preventative measure against disease; if you come down with an illness, I recommend that you see a doctor

3.

Bringing the Forest Indoors

Fill your house with plants

This might seem obvious, but there are many more reasons to bring plants indoors than simply to make your home look like a forest.

First, they help us to breathe. When we breathe in, we bring oxygen into our bodies. When we breathe out, we release carbon dioxide. Plants do the opposite: they absorb carbon dioxide and release oxygen. So having plants indoors increases the oxygen in our homes – and that is good for us. Oxygen affects every part of our bodies and making sure we get good-quality air is essential to our health.

Most plants switch at night and begin to absorb oxygen and release carbon dioxide, but not all plants do this. Some, like orchids and succulents, also release oxygen at night. These are good plants to fill your bedroom with so that oxygen levels stay high while you sleep.

Indoor air can be between two and five times as polluted as the air outdoors, and plants are natural air-purifiers. They act like sponges, soaking up the toxic chemicals found in paints, fabric, cigarettes and cleaning products. As part of a study that looked at ways to clean the air in space stations, NASA came up with a list of the top-ten air-purifying plants:

Peace lily

Golden pothos

English ivy

Chrysanthemum

Gerbera daisy

Mother-in-law's tongue

Bamboo palm

Azalea

Red-edge dracaena

Spider plant

The US Lung Institute recommends
putting Chinese evergreens and
areca palm in the living room,
gerbera daisies or snake plants in the
bedroom, and a money plant wherever
you like.

Because they raise the level of
humidity in the air, indoor plants
are also good at deterring illness.
The moisture they produce in the air
protects us from respiratory problems,
coughs and sore throats.

And, of course, plants in the home
make us feel calmer and happier and
fill our senses with beauty. We have
been making the indoors look like
outdoors for precisely this reason
since at least 610BC, when (so the
story goes) King Nebuchadnezzar
built the Hanging Gardens of Babylon
to comfort his wife, Amytis of Media,
because she missed the green hills and
lush gardens of her homeland.

The smell of outdoors inside

If you can't get outside for shinrin-yoku, you can bring the forest into your home with essential oils. I love to use *hinoki* oil, but there are many different oils you can use to create the wonderful woody atmosphere of the forest at home. All the conifer essential oils will remind you of the peace and quiet of the forest and bring you the powerful effects of a forest bath without you even having to leave the house.

You can bring the forest into your home with essential oils.

Here are some ways to get essential oils into your home.

1. Diffuser

Diffusers are a good alternative to candles. You don't breathe in any smoke and the oils stay in their original form. You just fill the diffuser with water and add a few drops of essential oil. The particles of oil are so small they stay in the air for several hours.

Diffusing oils is one of the most efficient ways to get essential oils into your body, and you can make up your own blend to create exactly the atmosphere and fragrance you want. This is my favourite way to bring the power of the forest directly into my home.

For a true Japanese forest-bathing experience, you can buy Japanese essential-oil blends that contain white cypress, hinoki wood and leaf, rosemary, cedar wood, eucalyptus and pine.

2. Reed diffuser

Reed diffusers work by absorbing the essential oil and releasing the aroma into the atmosphere. One end of the reeds sits in a mixture of essential oil and a carrier oil or clear alcohol. The essential oil is wicked up through the reeds and dispersed. Reed diffusers are very good for rooms where you can't plug in a diffuser, for example, the bathroom.

How to make a reed diffuser

What you need:

A small ceramic or glass jar or vase. Choose a container with a narrow opening at the top: the narrower the neck of the jar, the slower your oils will evaporate

Diffuser reeds or bamboo skewers – or some dried twigs, woody stems or reeds that will draw the liquid up. Your reeds should be about twice as tall as the container, so that they distribute the oil well

Essential oils of your choice

Carrier, or base, oil. For carrier oils, use a light vegetable oil like sweet almond oil, as heavier oils won't travel up the reeds so well. Or use clear alcohol, such as vodka, and some water

Directions:

1. If you are using an oil base, aim for 30 per cent essential oil to 70 per cent carrier oil; if you are using the alcohol and water mix, put 20–25 drops of essential oil in a quarter of a cup of hot water then add a few tablespoons of vodka

2. Pour the mixture into the container

3. Place the reeds in the bottle. Let the mixture saturate the reeds for a couple of hours. Then take them out and turn them round so that the saturated end is sticking out

4. Turn the reeds over once a week to renew the wonderful fragrance of the forest

5. Replace the reeds and refresh the mixture when you notice there is no longer any smell

3. Candles

You can fill your home with the smoky, warm fragrance of the Kiso valley with hinoki-scented candles. The traditional Japanese candle-making company Kodaikokuya makes a candle with the fragrance of native wild flowers as well as a Japanese-cypress-scented candle, so you can burn the two together to make your indoor forest bath smell just like a Japanese woodland.

Japanese candles are made from Japan wax, which comes from the sumac tree, whereas western candles tend to be made from petroleum. Japanese candles also have a different kind of wick. The wick in a western candle is made from thread, whereas the wick in a Japanese candle is made of rush grass. The grass reed is wrapped in washi paper and then dipped in wax. This creates a very bright and strong flame that will withstand a draught.

4. Cedarwood shavings

These will not only fill your house with the smell of a *hinoki* forest but will also keep moths and insects at bay. You can place bags of shavings in drawers and wardrobes to protect your clothes. A bowl of cedarwood shavings in your hallway will greet you with the smell of the forest every time you come home.

The ten virtues of Koh

Four hundred years ago, an unknown monk wrote out a list of the benefits of incense.

1. It brings communication with the transcendent

2. It refreshes the mind and body

3. It removes impurity

4. It awakens the spirit

5. It is a companion in solitude

6. It brings calm in turbulent times

7. Even in abundance, one never tires of it

8. Even in small amounts, it is sufficient

9. Age does not change its power

10. Used every day, it does no harm

Incense burners, like this one at the Sensō-ji temple in Tokyo, are common throughout Japan

The forest in your medicine cabinet

Many of our most common medicines come from trees. Did you know that the essential ingredient in aspirin comes from willow bark? The ancient Egyptians chewed it to reduce fevers. Hippocrates recommended making a tea from willow bark to ease pain and inflammation. Willow bark usually comes from the white willow tree. The inner and outer bark of the tree has different concentrations of compounds which are useful for different ailments, like stomach upsets or migraines.

All essential oils are antimicrobial, antifungal and antibacterial, and they are useful for a wide variety of everyday ailments, from bad breath to headaches, skin problems and stomach upsets.

Pine

Pine is one of the hardest-working forest oils in your medicine cupboard. An analgesic and anti-inflammatory, it can be mixed with a light vegetable oil and massaged into aching muscles and sore joints to relieve pain. Dermatologists sometimes prescribe it for itchy or sore skin, pimples and psoriasis. You can use pine to treat boils, cuts, scratches and sores, and its antifungal properties make it good for athlete's foot. Pine is said to be good if you have food poisoning because it speeds up the process with which the body eliminates toxins.

It is also a wonderful oil for colds and congested sinuses. When you're feeling under the weather, bring a pot of water to the boil. Remove from the stove and add three drops of pine oil and lean over the steam. Cover your head with a towel and inhale the steam through your mouth and nose.

You can also add drops of oil to a steaming hot bath or shower and breathe in its clearing scent. Steam inhalation of essential oils is a very direct method of aromatherapy and gets the phytoncides deep into the body.

A salt pipe or salt inhaler is another
very direct way of using essential oils
to help with a cold. A salt pipe is easy
to use. Just add the drops of oil to the
pipe and breathe in deeply through the
mouthpiece. The molecules of the oil are
absorbed from the salt and get deep into
your respiratory system. Pine, cypress
and fir oils are all good oils to put in a
salt inhaler.

Douglas fir

Douglas fir essential oil has cleaning and purifying properties when applied topically and is good to keep in your medicine cabinet as a cleanser. You can add it to your soaps and body washes for forest washing. It is very good for cleaning your house, too. To create a cleaner for floors and surfaces, fill a bucket with warm water and add two tablespoons of liquid soap, ten drops of Douglas fir essential oil, five drops of white fir and five drops of cypress.

Spruce

Spruce essential oil is another one that aromatherapists recommend for coughs and colds. Rub a couple of drops on your chest to help you breathe more easily. Spruce is also very good for treating wounds. It speeds up the healing process and prevents infection. Wash your cuts and grazes with water, and hydrogen peroxide if necessary, then swab with spruce essential oil on a clean cotton cloth.

Tea tree

Tea-tree oil doesn't actually come from a tree – it comes from an Australian shrub called *Melaleuca alternifolia* – but I'm including it here because it sounds like it comes from a tree and, like real tree oils, it is incredibly hard-working and has powerful antiseptic, antimicrobial and antifungal properties. To date, there are more than 327 scientific studies on its antimicrobial properties alone.

It can be used for cold sores, chicken-pox, ear aches, fungal infections, bad breath, head lice, dry cuticles, insect bites, sunburn, dandruff and acne. You can make a deodorant and a toothpaste by mixing tea-tree oil with coconut oil and baking soda. For a lotion for treating eczema, mix one teaspoon of coconut oil, five drops of tea-tree oil and five drops of lavender oil. You can even take your make-up off with it if you mix it with vegetable oil but be careful to avoid direct contact with the eyes.

WARNING:
Tea-tree oil is toxic when ingested.

Tea-tree oil actually comes from an Australian shrub called *Melaleuca alternifolia*

Fir needle

The ancient Egyptians massaged fir-needle oil into their scalps to promote scalp health and hair growth. Like all the conifer essential oils, it is a useful oil to have in the cupboard in winter. It is claimed that inhaling fir-needle oil can slow the progression of bacterial respiratory infections.

How to reset your body clock to forest time and get a good night's sleep

Humans evolved in a twenty-four-hour light/dark cycle known as the circadian clock. Ideally, we should wake in the morning when it gets light, have our faces bathed in natural light during the day and fall asleep when it gets dark. When we are exposed to light after the sun goes down, our bodies stay on daytime mode. Our heart rate goes up, our brains are more alert and our production of the sleep hormone melatonin is suppressed. These days, because we keep lights on in the dark evenings, our days have lengthened. We go to bed later and we don't get as much sleep.

And what is it that keeps us up the most? Our computer screens and phones and tablets; more specifically, the glow of the screen and the type of light it emits. Studies show that reading a tablet or smart phone for a couple of hours before bedtime can delay sleep by about an hour.

The American Medical Association
Council on Science and Public Health has
said that 'exposure to excessive light at
night, including extended use of various
electronic media, can disrupt sleep or
exacerbate sleep disorders, especially in
children and adolescents'.

Teenagers are twice as sensitive to light
at night as older people. So, manipulating
lighting is key to good health.

At home, we can do various things to reduce the amount of artificial light in our lives and to help bring our bodies into harmony with natural light patterns.

- Switch off any lights you are not using

- Install smart lighting. This is lighting that you can alter according to the light of the day, reducing the brightness and changing the colour emitted, from blue light for daytime to the warm light of the evening. You can programme the lights to turn on and off at pre-set times. Smart lighting can be set to function as an alarm and come on to wake you up gently in the morning. This is still quite new technology, but it is a step in the right direction

- Remove all blue light from your environment when the sun goes down. To do this, use a light app like f.lux, which alters the light of your computer screen to suit the time of day. The developers of f.lux say, 'During the day, computer screens look good – they're designed to look like the sun. But at 9 p.m., 10 p.m. or 3 a.m., you probably shouldn't be looking at the sun.' Twilight is another great app for managing the light from your device.

- I do radio gymnastic exercises or t'ai chi outdoors in the morning. You might like to try green yoga in the park, like we do in some of the forest bases in Japan

- Go for a two-night/three-day forest-bathing trip. Spending two nights in the forest, living with a natural light schedule, will synchronize your biological clock with forest time and restore your natural cycle to help you get a good night's sleep

Green exercise

Studies from the University
of Essex (UK) have found that
exercising outside surrounded
by green makes us happier,
less tired and gives us a longer-
lasting energy boost than when
we exercise indoors.

Researchers found that
exercising outside makes us
feel better about ourselves than
when we exercise indoors,
and that the results of green
exercise can be felt very quickly.
You don't have to go for a long
hike up a mountain before
you feel better. Even very short
bouts of outdoor exercise can
have a big impact on our mood.

Exercising outdoors is also easier.
Or rather, we perceive that it
is easier. When we exercise in
environments that we find attractive,
it feels less arduous. A brisk walk
outside will seem much easier than
a walk on a treadmill in a gym,
although we may have walked just
as far.

And when we enjoy an activity, we
are much more likely to want to do
it again. Research shows that we are
better at sticking to our exercise
regimes when we exercise outside
– and anything that increases
the likelihood that we'll carry on
exercising is a good thing.

You don't have to get into the
forest to do green exercise. Any
natural environment is good for
you, including city parks. Exercising
where you can see the colour blue
as well as the colour green seems
to confer the greatest benefits. So, if
you can go for your green exercise
where there is some water, that's
even better.

How to forest-bathe at work

The average office worker spends about 1,600 hours a year at work. That is around 35 per cent of your waking hours in the course of a fifty-year working life so, to keep the connection between us and nature while we're at work, it is vital to incorporate the natural world into our work environment.

Productive plants

Plants are key to a healthy environment in offices. Bringing nature into our workspaces doesn't just make us feel better, it actually improves our health. In offices with plants, there is not just an increase in morale but a decrease in sick leave and absenteeism. Plants have been proved to reduce the general feelings of ill health associated with Sick Building Syndrome – dry and itchy skin, sore throats and headaches, lethargy, irritability and poor concentration. And like the plants we bring into our homes, the plants in our offices will get rid of the toxins in the air released by carpets, printers and upholstery.

Plants also help keep up humidity levels in our offices. Dry air causes respiratory problems and skin irritation, and offices have low humidity levels caused by air conditioning and heating. The air indoors is also low in negative ions (those are the good ones) – electronic equipment sucks them out – but plants can put them back. This does more than help with afternoon headaches and feelings of sluggishness. If you have ever had the suspicion that you catch more colds when you are in an air-conditioned office, you are right. Negative ions given off by the plants will purify the air and make it healthier to breathe. Negative ions bond with, and remove, dust particles, mould, bacteria and allergens in the air. They get rid of the germs.

So, it's no wonder that people who have plants in their offices are more energized, feel less stressed and are better able to concentrate. We are more productive, more efficient and more creative when we work where there are plants. Not having plants in the workplace is associated with higher levels of tension and anxiety.

We are more productive, more efficient and more creative when we work where there are plants.

If you can't bring a tree into your office, bring in some of the plants on NASA's list (see p. 228) for your windowsill or desk, or put them on a shelf. The peace lily needs nothing much more than overhead lighting and weekly watering. The snake plant also thrives in low light and with little water and will filter out carbon dioxide and formaldehyde. One of the easiest plants to look after is bamboo. It doesn't need sunlight; in fact, it doesn't even need soil. Just put it in a little water and it will be fine.

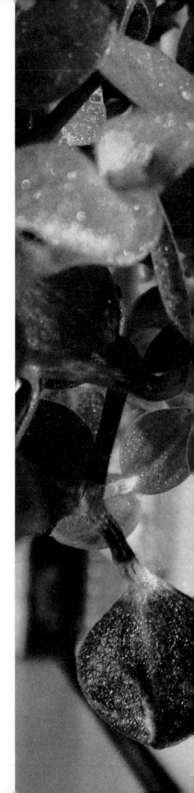

Outdoor sounds

We know that listening to the sounds
of the natural world has a restorative
effect on our cognitive abilities when
we are in the forest, so it is not
surprising that studies have found that
listening to the sounds of nature when
we are at work can help us to focus and
get more done.

Findings presented at the Acoustical
Society of America in 2015 showed that
listening to the sounds of nature not
only helps us to be more productive
but also makes us feel more positive
about our work environment. People
reported feeling happier when they
could hear the sounds of nature in
their office than when office noise
was blocked with white noise or when
there was no sound at all.

There are many recordings of forest
sounds on YouTube. Right now, I am
listening to birdsong, a babbling brook
and the wind in the leaves. If you
long for the restorative quiet of the
Hoh Rainforest in Olympic National
Park, the one-square-inch project
(www.onesquareinch.org) has made a
recording of the natural silence there.
You can play this in your office to
block out irritating noise and help you
concentrate. Maybe, one day, all offices
will sound like this.

Take a green micro-break

If, like me, you have a view of nature from your
window at work, you will know how much
better it can make you feel – and how lucky
you are. I can enjoy shinrin-yoku from my
window every day. Looking out at the trees,
seeing what the birds are doing and watching
the seasons change helps me to concentrate
and to keep up my focus throughout the day.
Several studies have shown that having a view
of nature through a window makes people
feel better about their jobs and reduces
job-related stress.

But now, research from the University of
Melbourne has shown that all it takes is a
'green micro-break' to restore us when we
are mentally fatigued. The study found that it
can take as little as forty seconds of looking
out of the window at a natural scene to help
us focus and stay alert. Other research, from
the University of Rochester in New York state,
demonstrates that just a brief glimpse of the
colour green before doing a creative task is
enough to enhance creative performance.
Researchers from the University of Michigan
psychology department have shown that taking
ten minutes to look at pictures of nature is
enough to improve cognitive performance.

If you don't have a window to
look out of, any kind of pictures
of nature and green vegetation will
help. So have a picture of nature as a
screensaver on your computer, or as
the lock screen on your phone. Pin
photographs of the countryside on
the wall near your desk. And, when
you take a break, just sit back and
enjoy them.

Go barefoot

Only joking! But reconnecting to the earth's electrical charge, in the way I talked about in Chapter 2, is possible indoors – even if you keep your shoes on. You can use a variety of products that conduct the earth's charge when you are at work. There are grounding mats, bands and sheets, all of which conduct the electrons from the earth into your body and keep you connected to the ground, no matter how high up your office is. A grounding desk mat, for example, simply plugs in and goes under your computer, or it can be used as a mouse mat.

If you do want to take your shoes off, you can get a grounding mat to go underneath your desk. Plug it in, take off your shoes and socks and put your bare feet on the mat. You might feel all the benefits of walking barefoot in the forest!

The fragrant workplace

We saw in Chapter 1 how two nurses diffused essential oils throughout their busy emergency department to manage stress among the staff. Research has also been carried out in Taiwan that shows how helpful diffusing essential oils can be to exhausted primary-school teachers. Wherever you work, essential oils can help.

If you want the smell of the forest in your office, all the evergreen essential oils can be good when energy is flagging. They will help fight fatigue, relieve tension and anxiety and improve concentration. They are especially good in the winter months when we need extra support for our immune systems. My work room smells of hinoki all winter long.

Take a forest bath in the local park

The best way to deal with stress
at work is to go for a forest
bath. I go for shinrin-yoku every
lunchtime. You don't need a
forest; any small green space will
do. Leave your cup of coffee and
your phone behind and just walk
slowly. You don't need to exercise,
you just need to open your
senses to nature. It will improve
your mood, reduce tension and
anxiety, and help you focus and
concentrate for the rest of the day.

The Retiro Park is one of Madrid's
finest green spaces

Kimiya's story

I go to many parks in Tokyo for shinrin-yoku. My favourite park is Arisugawa-no-Miya Memorial Park. There is a river in the park, as well as forest. All of nature is here, even though the park is small.

I hadn't heard about shinrin-yoku before I started my medical studies. I was surprised to learn that walking in the forest could have such beneficial effects on our health and that phytoncides can relax us and help us to de-stress.

I was very stressed at the time that I did forest-bathing with my class, but I could feel the relaxing effects, and my scores on the questionnaires about mood were always improved at the end of the walk.

When I am not stressed, I communicate better with my family and my friends, so I think shinrin-yoku is helpful for my relationships.

Haruka's story

I love to go to the park and feel the sunshine during the day. It makes me feel very relaxed.

Of all the parks we go to, the one I like best is Showa Memorial Park. This is a park outside Tokyo, full of tall trees and grass rather than high buildings, people and cars. When I walk in Showa Kinen Park, I feel very free. Because I am a medical student, I have to study hard every day and don't have much time to relax. To go to the park and experience shinrin-yoku is a very precious time for me.

4.

Thinking about the Future

The key to preserving our forests for the future

A few facts:

- Forests cover 31 per cent of the world's land

- Over 1.6 billion people depend on forests for their livelihood, and some 300 million people live in them

- Forests contain 80 per cent of the world's land biodiversity and are home to 60,000 different types of trees

- And they store more than 1 trillion tonnes of carbon, twice the amount found in the atmosphere

These are some of the things that the United Nations reminded us of when they proclaimed the International Year of Forests in 2011. This was a campaign to highlight the role of all types of forests in our lives. Forest 2011 was themed as 'Forests for People' and its aim was to bring people all over the world together in forest-related activities to strengthen our connection to forests everywhere and remind us how important they are for our health and well-being.

The following year, the UN declared 21 March International Forest Day. There has been an International Forest Day every 21 March since then, with countries across the world taking part in campaigns and events to celebrate and raise awareness of the importance of trees and forests in our lives, not just now but for future generations.

Never has it been more important
to maintain and strengthen our
relationship with forests and to remind
us that they help us. Each year, more
than 32 million acres of forest are lost
across the world. That is an area around
the size of England. While I am writing
this sentence, another 7.5 acres will have
been lost. By the end of the day, 88,000
acres will have disappeared.

Let's put it another way. One study found
that there are around 3.04 trillion trees
on earth. That's around 400 for each
person on the planet. And 15 billion are
lost every year – or around 2 trees per
person. That's a lot of trees. In fact, we've
nearly halved the amount of trees there
are on the planet.

And as we lose trees, so the benefits
they provide to our health are lost. As
I've shown you in this book, forests
reduce our stress, boost our immune
system and help us to live longer, better
and happier lives. Our health and the
health of the forest go hand in hand.
When trees die, we die. If our forests
are unhealthy, then so are we. You can't
have a healthy population without
healthy forests.

The key to preserving our forest,
wherever it is, is to maintain our
connection with it, and one of the best
ways to do that is to remind people
that our health and the health of our
communities depends on it. When we
feel connected to nature, we want to
look after it. And this in turn is good for
our health. We will benefit not just from
the clean air and water forests provide,
the carbon they store, the species they
maintain, but also from the peace and
quiet they offer, their beauty and vital
spirit, and the myriad benefits to our
well-being they hold within them.

Our health
and the
health of
the forest
go hand in
hand.

I can't think of a better way to establish our connection to the forest, to feel its power and importance for ourselves, than to go for a forest bath. When you are intimately connected to the forest through all five of your senses – when you can feel the warm breeze on your skin, hear the motion of the leaves in the trees, smell for yourself the fragrance of the trees, taste the delicious fresh air, and let your mind be captured by all the beauty of the natural world – you feel restored and refreshed. The forest can bring you back to health and life, and you will want to conserve and protect it in turn.

When we love nature, we are likely to look after it. The more we connect with the natural world, the more likely we are to preserve it for the future.

When you are intimately connected to the forest through all five of your senses, you feel restored and refreshed.

The future of forest medicine

The future of shinrin-yoku

Forest-bathing is now a standard practice in Japan. There are sixty-two forest bases and roads across the country, all designated healing forests and each with a particular healing feature. In Kunigami, in tropical northern Okinawa, you can feel the *yanbaru-no-mori*, the subtropical natural environment, on your skin. In Chizu, Tottori, flows one of the best streams in Japan. Akasawa has the intense special fragrance of the *hinoki* trees. Experts in forests and health care are on hand in many of our bases to help you to connect with nature through all five of your senses and to make the most of its restorative powers. In some of our forest bases, you can be accompanied by a doctor as you walk or have your blood pressure checked in cabins along the trail.

And Japan is not the only country where this is happening. There are organizations across the world which are conducting research, sharing information and providing platforms for governments, universities, corporations and businesses to understand the impact the forest has on our health and to implement strategies so that both we and the forests can benefit.

The village of Chizu is also home to the Ishitani Residence, which boasts some exquisite gardens

Scratch the surface, and you will find a plethora of organizations whose aim is to strengthen and develop the connection between us and the natural world, for our health and the health of our communities, as well as the health of the planet.

Indeed, doctors throughout the world are now prescribing spending time in nature rather than a pill for a wide range of ailments and conditions, from addictions and depression to high blood pressure, obesity and diabetes. New Zealand has long boasted a 'green prescription' scheme, and many other countries are looking to follow suit. The National ParkRx initiative in America has been encouraging citizens to use the forests, parks and trails to improve their health since 2009. There are now more than 150 park-prescription programmes in America, in states from Alabama to Wisconsin, through which people can reap the health benefits of being in nature – and learn to look after the countryside in turn. And in 2015, nature organizations in the UK called for 1 per cent of the National Health budget to be spent on improving people's access to green spaces and the coastline, for the good of the nation's health.

One of the most ambitious forest medicine programmes in the world is in South Korea. The South Korean government has spent more than $14 million on a National Forest Therapy Centre, has developed thirty-seven state-run recreational forests, and is training five hundred forest-healing instructors.

The National Forest Plan is to create a 'green welfare state, where forests bring happiness to everyone', at every stage of life. The forests in South Korea offer everything from prenatal classes to forest kindergarten and burial services. They are places where people can live, work and play, from the cradle to the grave.

The future of our urban forests

Preserving our urban forests is just as important as looking after our tropical and wild forests and woodlands. Trees are a vital and integral part of our urban lives, as important a part of a city's infrastructure as roads and broadband – and much more beautiful than either. They remove tonnes of pollution, store tonnes of carbon and help mitigate extreme temperatures. Their root systems absorb water and help with excess rainfall. They provide respite and relief from noise and dirt, boost our immune systems and relieve our stress.

As trees are lost to developments, buildings and roads, and to insects, diseases and storms, there is an ever-pressing need for us to remember everything that the urban forest can do for us. In 2015, the World Economic Forum made increasing green canopy cover one of its top-ten urban initiatives and, across the world, there are movements to encourage cities to plant more trees and increase their green spaces.

The story of Tokyo's street trees

The first disaster to hit Tokyo's urban forest
in the last century was a typhoon in 1917
in which more than half the city's trees were
lost. In 1923, the Kanton earthquake led to a
further loss of trees, reducing their number by
about 60 per cent.

The urban forest was further devastated by
the American firebombing of the city in the
Second World War. Around 160km² of Tokyo
were burned and the number of trees fell
from 105,000 to 42,000. And, in the years
immediately after the war, an additional
10 per cent of the trees that remained were
lost. Some became diseased and died; others
were cut down for firewood.

Several of those few that survived are now
among Tokyo's most special trees — silent
witnesses to what happened to the city during
the years of the Second World War.

New trees began to be planted in 1946, and
barren parts of the city were earmarked to have
new green spaces. But it wasn't until 1959

and the decision to host the 1964 Olympic
Games in Tokyo that any real effort was made
to re-green the city. Tree-lined boulevards were
created and many streets widened so that trees
could be planted. By 1980, there were more
than 235,000 trees on Tokyo's streets.

The project for Green Tokyo was launched
in 2006. This aimed to bring the number of
street trees up to 1 million and to add another
1,000 hectares of green space to the city,
including a woodland park on a landfill site
on an island in the Bay of Tokyo, to be known
as Umi-no-mori, or the Sea Forest. Today, the
surface of Umi-no-mori is already green with
grass and trees. It will be open for the next
Tokyo Olympics, which will take place
in 2020.

Amazingly, in a recent survey of tree density
in megacities, Tokyo was found to have the
highest tree canopy cover per person, more
than Mumbai, London, Moscow, Mexico City,
Beijing and Buenos Aires.

Which cities in the world have the most green space?

10. Los Angeles, California – 15.2%

9. Tel Aviv, Israel – 17.5%

8. Boston, Massachusetts – 18.2%

7. Miami, Florida – 19.4%

6. Toronto, Canada – 19.5%

5. Seattle, Washington – 20%

4. Frankfurt, Germany – 21.5%

3. Sacramento, California – 23.6%

2. Vancouver, Canada – 25.9%

1. Singapore – 29.3%

I took these figures from a website called Treepedia, a collection of interactive maps that show the density of trees in major cities around the world and which the website designers hope individuals, as well as governments, will use to see how green their cities are – or not; and where they are not green, encourage them to plant trees and green them up.

According to a recent survey Tokyo now has one of the highest tree canopy covers per person

The developers used Google Street View rather than satellite imagery, so when you click on a map you can see how green a city is at street level. What another tree-mapping tool, iTree, has revealed, however, is that much of a city's urban forest is actually in its private gardens, on its golf courses, on railway embankments and in cemeteries. When it measured London, the iTree urban-forest survey found that 60 per cent of its trees are in Londoners' gardens. And that one of the city's most common tree species is in fact the apple tree — not a tree you see often when you walk down London's streets!

This just goes to show how important our individual contributions to the urban forest are. Every tree counts, even if it's only an apple tree in your back garden — and it counts in financial terms, too. iTree maps the monetary value of the 'eco services' that trees provide — the carbon they store, the pollution they remove, the amount of storm-water run-off they reduce. As noted earlier, it calculated that the 8.4 million trees in London provide £133 million in benefits each year.

The US Forest Service has calculated that trees in American cities remove $3.8 billion worth of air pollution, prevent 670,000 incidents of acute respiratory symptoms and save 850 lives a year. Figures from Washington DC show that the amount of pollution trees remove in the city is the equivalent of taking 274,000 cars off the roads. That is a saving of about $51 million a year in pollution-related health care costs.

Many cities have strategies in place to increase the size of their urban forests. In 2003, Adelaide, South Australia, put in place a plan to plant 3 million trees and shrubs by 2014. Melbourne plans to increase the city's tree canopy from 22 per cent to 40 per cent by 2040. San Francisco has mapped 37 neighbourhoods, inventoried 124,847 trees and located spaces for planting 39,688 more trees, as well as calculating the $2,333,450 the city's trees already provide in annual eco benefits. Trees for Cities has already planted 75,000 urban trees across the world and is aiming to plant 1 million by 2020. In Northern Ireland, 200,000 trees have been planted since the end of the Troubles in 1998, and the One Million Trees in One Day scheme has planted 730,000 native trees at more than 3,000 sites in Ireland and Northern Ireland since 2013.

Singapore, already the greenest city in the world, is aiming to make itself even greener. Its goal is for 85 per cent of its residents to live within 400 metres of a green space. If all cities made themselves this green, just think how many more of us would lead healthier and happier lives.

As cities become more crowded they also have to become more innovative about how they create more green space. Inspired by New York's regeneration of its High Line railway, and the beautiful Promenade Plantée in Paris, which converted the old Vincennes railway into nearly 5km of green walkway ten metres above the street, cities across the world are turning their old motorways and railways into parks and green spaces.

Philadelphia has begun to green up a 5km stretch of disused rail track that runs across its Center City District. Washington DC is planting trees and meadows and building waterfalls on top of four piers that once supported the 11th Street Bridge. The 606 Park in Chicago will transform a nearly 4.5km stretch of railway line into lush gardens. Singapore has a plan to transform the Keretapi Tanah Melayu railway track that used to connect it to Malaysia into a new Green Corridor.

Skygarden in Seoul has been built
on an abandoned motorway flyover.
The concrete overpass has been
planted with what the architects
call a 'library' of 24,000 shrubs
and trees, all arranged according to
the Korean alphabet, in a pattern
designed to bring out their colour
contrasts. Skygarden is open
twenty-four hours a day, like a real
forest. At night, blue light wraps
itself around the plants so that it's
'as if you're walking in a cosmos'.

Seoul's Skygarden is built on
a former inner-city highway

Our children, the future

As more and more of us have moved
into the city, fewer and fewer of our
children have the access to nature that
we had, or that their grandparents had.
Our children do not know the wide
variety of plants that was common
not so long ago and which is fast
disappearing. I wonder if they know
how to tell which of the elm-tree leaves
are good to eat, like I knew when I was
a child, or if they have ever seen an
apricot tree in full bloom.

In *Last Child in the Woods*, Richard Louv
came up with a term to describe the
gap between children and nature. He
called it a 'nature deficit disorder',
and he has linked the lack of nature
in young people's lives to the rise in
behavioural disorders, depression
and obesity, in addition to the lack of
vitamin D and the increase in short-
sightedness that we see when children
don't spend enough time outdoors.

Louv tells us that it is not so much what children know about the natural world that is important as what happens to them when they are in it! Children learn better outdoors. And they are better behaved. When children with ADHD are exposed to nature, their symptoms disappear. Nature is good for their mental and physical development. They are less likely to become ill or stressed if they spend time outside. And they are happier, reporting that playing outdoors gives them more pleasure than playing on electronic devices. Of course, our children need to know about the natural world, but they also need to get outside, just for the joy of it. They need to get their feet muddy and their hands dirty, just for fun.

Nature is good for children's mental and physical development.

As the American Medical Association put it as long ago as 2005, 'Children will be smarter, better able to get along with each other, healthier and happier when they have regular opportunities for free and unstructured play in the out-of-doors.'

Most importantly, if children play out-of-doors, they will grow up to look after it. A growing body of evidence shows that being in nature when we are young creates a sense of connection with the natural world that lasts as we grow up. Children who have fun in nature will become adults who care for and protect it and understand its importance. If we let our children play outside now, they will become the green architects of the future, the green city-planners and tree-mappers, the gardeners, nature therapists and forest-medicine doctors!

Many people believe that connecting children with nature should be a fundamental part of their education, for their cognitive development, their psychological and physical health and for the health of the future. In many places, this is already happening. Schools across the world are expanding their classrooms to include parks and green spaces. Children are being taken outside not just to learn about nature but to learn when they are in it – even in big cities like London, New York and Berlin.

Even in Japan, where educational pressure is intense and rules are strict, there are a growing number of forest kindergartens, or *mori-no-ie*, where children are taught outside, whatever the weather.

But perhaps, when you think about it, this is not so surprising after all. The connection with nature is such an important part of Japanese culture. In a forest kindergarten, children spend five days a week having forest adventures – mori-no-tanken – climbing mountains and trees, getting their hands dirty and their feet muddy. Playing outside every day helps them to learn resilience and independence, to develop confidence and creativity. But most importantly, it helps them to learn to love the beautiful landscape of Japan. And their love of the countryside will be their most important environmental skill.

All the research shows that we will look after what we love. If we give our children these experiences, they will love the places in the forest where they played and learned. If we let our young people engage with the beauty of the natural world they will learn to love and understand its spirit. In the end, it is our children's relationship with the natural world that determines its future. If we let our children go into the forest, they will become adults who will protect it.

If we let our children go into the forest, they will become adults who will protect it.

40 BEAUTIFUL FORESTS ACROSS THE WORLD

Kellerwald-Edersee, Germany

Ardennes, Belgium

Amsterdamse Bos, Netherlands

Caledonian Forest, Cairngorms National Park, Scotland, UK

Black Forest, Germany

Wistman's Wood, Dartmoor, UK

New Forest, UK

Mastbos, Netherlands

Killarney National Park, Ireland

Tongass Forest, Alaska, USA

Acadian Forest, Canada

Cévennes National Park, France

Boreal Forest, Canada

Cork Oak Forests, Alentejo, Portugal

Humboldt Redwoods State Park, California, USA

Pyrénées National Park, Midi-Pyrénées, France

Salmon-Challis, Idaho, USA

La Palma, Canaries

Corcovado National Park, Costa Rica

Azrou Cedar Forest, Morocco

Green Mountain National Forest, Vermont, USA

Bosco Archiforo, Calabria, Italy

White Mountains, New Hampshire, USA

San Vito Cork Oak Forest, Lazio, Italy

Amazon Rainforest, South America

Aggtelek National Park, Hungary

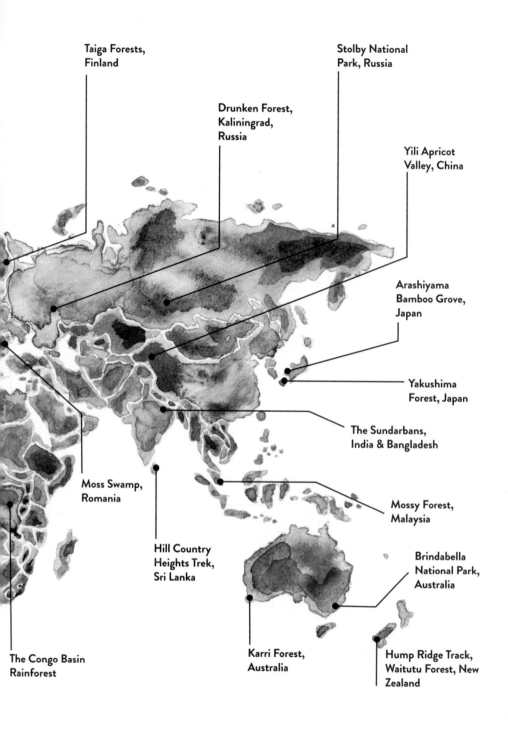

Taiga Forests,
Finland

Stolby National
Park, Russia

Drunken Forest,
Kaliningrad,
Russia

Yili Apricot
Valley, China

Arashiyama
Bamboo Grove,
Japan

Yakushima
Forest, Japan

The Sundarbans,
India & Bangladesh

Moss Swamp,
Romania

Mossy Forest,
Malaysia

Hill Country
Heights Trek,
Sri Lanka

Brindabella
National Park,
Australia

The Congo Basin
Rainforest

Karri Forest,
Australia

Hump Ridge Track,
Waitutu Forest, New
Zealand

The POMS Test

The POMS (Profile of Mood States) questionnaire is a tool widely used to measure psychological well-being. It was developed in 1971 by Douglas M. McNair, along with Maurice Lorr and Leo F. Droppleman. There are several versions of the questionnaire. The most commonly used is the POMS 2. It is available as a full-length questionnaire (65 items) and in a shorter version (34 items).

The one I use is an adaptation of a version designed by Dr J. R. Grove at the University of Western Australia.

You should complete this questionnaire twice – before and after your forest-bathing trip – and compare your scores. (NB: a lot of these emotions seem to be the same: that's deliberate! They are nuances of six particular mood scales, as you'll discover in the scoring section.)

	NOT AT ALL	A LITTLE	MODERATELY	QUITE A LOT	EXTREMELY		SCALE
Tense	0	1	2	3	4		ANX
Angry	0	1	2	3	4		ANG
Worn-out	0	1	2	3	4		FAT
Unhappy	0	1	2	3	4		DEP
Lively	0	1	2	3	4		VIG
Confused	0	1	2	3	4		CON
Sad	0	1	2	3	4		DEP
Active	0	1	2	3	4		VIG
On edge	0	1	2	3	4		ANX
Grumpy	0	1	2	3	4		ANG
Energetic	0	1	2	3	4		VIG
Lacking in hope	0	1	2	3	4		DEP
Uneasy	0	1	2	3	4		ANX
Restless	0	1	2	3	4		ANX
Unable to concentrate	0	1	2	3	4		CON
Fatigued	0	1	2	3	4		FAT
Annoyed	0	1	2	3	4		ANG
Discouraged	0	1	2	3	4		DEP
Resentful	0	1	2	3	4		ANG
Nervous	0	1	2	3	4		ANX
Miserable	0	1	2	3	4		DEP
Bitter	0	1	2	3	4		ANG
Exhausted	0	1	2	3	4		FAT
Anxious	0	1	2	3	4		ANX
Helpless	0	1	2	3	4		DEP
Weary	0	1	2	3	4		FAT
Energized	0	1	2	3	4		VIG
Bewildered	0	1	2	3	4		CON
Furious	0	1	2	3	4		VIG
Worthless	0	1	2	3	4		DEP
Forgetful	0	1	2	3	4		CON
Vigorous	0	1	2	3	4		VIG
Uncertain about things	0	1	2	3	4		CON
Drained	0	1	2	3	4		FAT

Each of these emotions falls into a particular mood scale. Add up your total scores for each scale to get your results for before and after your forest-bathing trip.

ANX = anxiety	Mark out of 24
DEP = depression	Mark out of 28
ANG = anger	Mark out of 20
VIG = vigour	Mark out of 24
FAT = fatigue	Mark out of 20
CON = confusion	Mark out of 20

Studies referred to in this book

INTRODUCTION: Our Relationship to Forests

p. 14 *The Biophilia Hypothesis*, S. R. Kellert and E. O. Wilson (eds.), 1993
p. 35 The Total Audience Report: QI 2016, The Nielsen Company
p. 35 Communications Market Report, Ofcom, 2014

1. From a Feeling to a Science

p. 70 Study group led by Y. Miyazaki, Chiba University
p. 72 'A Before-and-after Comparison of the Effects of Forest Walking on the Sleep of a Community-based Sample of People with Sleep Complaints', E. Morita et al, 2011
pp. 94–8 'Effect of Hinoki and Meniki Essential Oils on Human Autonomic Nervous System Activity and Mood States', C. J. Chen et al, 2015; 'Physiological Effect of Olfactory Stimulation by Hinoki Cypress (*Chamaecyparis obtusa*) Leaf Oil', Harumi Ikei et al, 2015
p. 99 'Effects of Citrus Fragrance on Immune Function and Depressive States', T. Komori et al, 1995
pp. 99–101 Tonya McBride and Teresa Sturges, *Living Magazine*, autumn 2012
p. 102 'SRL172 (Killed *Mycobacterium vaccae*) in Addition to Standard Chemotherapy Improves Quality of Life without Affecting Survival, in Patients with Advanced Non-small-cell Lung Cancer: Phase 3 Results', M. E. O'Brien et al, 2004
pp. 102–3 'Identification of an Immune-responsive Mesolimbocortical Serotonergic System: Potential Role in Regulation of Emotional Behaviour', C. A. Lowry et al, 2007
p. 105 'The Cognitive Benefits of Interacting with Nature', Marc G. Berman, John Jonides and Stephen Kaplan, 2008
p. 105 'Nature Experience Reduces Rumination and Subgenus Prefrontal Cortex Activation', Gregory N. Bratman et al, 2015

p. 106 'Creativity in the Wild: Improving Creative Reasoning Through Immersion in Natural Settings', Ruth Ann Atchley, David L. Strayer and Paul Atchley, 2012
p. 108 'An Occasion for Unselfing: Beautiful Nature Leads to Prosociality', Jia Wei Zhang et al, 2013; 'Awe, the Small Self and Prosocial Behaviour', Paul K. Piff et al, 2015; 'Can Nature Make Us More Caring? Effects of Immersion in Nature on Intrinsic Aspirations and Generosity', Netta Weinstein, Andrew K. Przybylski and Richard R. Ryan, 2009
p. 109 'Positive Affect and Markers of Inflammation: Discrete Positive Emotions Predict Lower Levels of Inflammatory Cytokines', Jennifer E. Stellar et al, 2015
p. 111 'View through a Window May Influence Recovery from Surgery', Roger S. Ulrich, 1984
p. 114 'The Relationship between Trees and Human Health: Evidence from the Spread of the Emerald Ash Borer', G. H. Donovan et al, 2013
p. 115 'Would You be Happier Living in a Greener Urban Area? A Fixed-effects Analysis of Panel Data', Mathew P. White et al, 2013
p. 115 'Urban Street Tree Density and Antidepressant Prescription Rates: A Cross-sectional Study in London, UK', Mark S. Taylor et al, 2015
p. 116 'Neighborhood Greenspace and Health in a Large Urban Center', Omid Kardan et al, 2015
p. 116 'Urban Residential Environments and Senior Citizens' Longevity in Megacity Areas: The Importance of Walkable Green Spaces', T. Takano, K. Nakamura Takano and M. Watanabe, 2002

2. How to Practise Shinrin-Yoku

p. 163 'Mind-wandering and Alternations to Default Mode Network Connectivity when Listening to Naturalistic versus Artificial Sounds', Cassandra D. Gould van Praag et al, 2017

p. 165 'Inducing Physiological Stress Recovery with Sounds of Nature in a Virtual Reality Forest: Results from a Pilot Study', Matilda Annerstedt et al, 2013
p. 176 'Fractal Patterns in Nature and Art are Aesthetically Pleasing and Stress-reducing', Richard Taylor, *The Conversation*, 2017
p. 223 'Happiness and Feeling Connected: The Distinct Role of Nature Relatedness', John M. Zelenski and Elizabeth K. Nisbet, 2012

3. Bringing the Forest Indoors

p. 244 Draxe.com
p. 245 Drericz.com
p. 252 'What is the Best Dose of Nature and Green Exercise for Improving Mental Health? A Multi-study Analysis', Jo Barton and Jules Pretty, 2010
p. 260 'Natural Sounds Improve Mood and Productivity', Acoustical Society of America, 2015
p. 262 'The Influence of Forest View through a Window on Job Satisfaction and Job Stress', Won Sop Shin, 2007; 'The Role of Nature in the Context of the Workplace', Rachel Kaplan, 1993
p. 262 '40-second Green Roof Views Sustain Attention: The Role of Micro-breaks in Attention Restoration', Kate E. Lee et al, 2015
p. 262 'Fertile Green: Green Facilitates Creative Performance', Stephanie Lichtenfeld, Andrew J. Elliot and Markus A. Maier, 2012
p. 262 'The Cognitive Benefits of Interacting with Nature', Marc G. Berman, John Jonides and Stephen Kaplan, 2008
p. 268 'Aromatherapy Benefits Autonomic Nervous System Regulation for Elementary School Faculty in Taiwan', Kang-Ming Chang and Chuh-Wei Shen, 2011

4. Thinking about the Future

p. 296 *Last Child in the Woods*, Richard Louv, 2005

Further Reading

Websites

www.childrenandnature.org: Richard Louv's organization 'to fuel the worldwide grassroots movement to reconnect children with nature'

www.fo-society.jp: Forest Medicine Therapy Society in Japan

www.forest-medicine.com: The Society for Forest Medicine in Japan

www.greenexercise.org: the home of green exercise research at the University of Essex, UK

www.hphpcentral.com: the Healthy Parks Healthy People organization in the United States, which aims to bring together 'the latest international research, innovations and programs that focus on the health benefits of human contact with the natural world'

www.infom.org: International Society of Nature and Forest Medicine

www.natureandforesttherapy.org: an American-based organization whose mission is 'to mobilize healthcare networks to connect people with nature', offering guide training, workshops and retreats.

www.onesquareinch.org: the research project in the Hoh Rainforest of Olympic National Park, US

www.shinrin-yoku.org: a member of the Association of Nature and Forest Therapy Guides and Programs, offering guide training and with a useful handbook for guides, *A Little Handbook of Shinrin-Yoku*, by M. Amos Clifford

Books

Li, Qing, *Forest Medicine*, 2012

Louv, Richard, *The Nature Principle: Reconnecting with Life in a Virtual Age*, 2012,

  Last Child in the Woods, 2005

Selhub, Eva M., and Alan C. Logan, *Your Brain on Nature: The Science of Nature's Influence on Your Health, Happiness and Vitality*, 2014

Williams, Florence, *The Nature Fix: Why Nature Makes Us Happier, Healthier and More Creative*, 2017

Picture Permissions

Acknowledgements

My research was supported partly by a
research project for utilizing advanced
technologies in agriculture, forestry and
the fisheries of Japan, and by Grants-
in-Aid for Scientific Research from the
Ministry of Education, Culture, Sports,
Science and Technology in Japan.

I am grateful to the staff at the Department
of Hygiene and Public Health, Nippon
Medical School, for their assistance.

Thank you to the team at Penguin Life
who worked on this book, and to Anna
Vaux for helping me bring my research to
the page.